04207222

GETTIN(

How To Books on Jobs and Careers

Applying for a Job
Career Networking
Career Planning for Women
Doing Voluntary Work Abroad
Finding a Job in Canada
Finding a Job in Computers
Finding a Job with a Future
Finding Work Overseas
Freelance DJ-ing
Freelance Teaching & Tutoring
Getting a Job After University
Getting a Job in America
Getting into Films & Television
Getting that Job
Getting Your First Job
How to Be a Freelance Journalist
How to Be a Freelance Sales Agent
How to Be a Freelance Secretary
How to Become an Au Pair
How to Find Temporary Work
 Abroad
How to Get a Job Abroad
How to Get a Job in Australia
How to Get a Job in Europe
How to Get a Job in France

How to Get a Job in Germany
How to Get a Job in Travel &
 Tourism
How to Get Into Radio
How to Know Your Rights at Work
How to Manage Your Career
How to Market Yourself
How to Return to Work
How to Start a New Career
How to Work from Home
How to Work in an Office
How to Work in Retail
How to Work with Dogs
How to Write a CV That Works
Living & Working in China
Passing That Interview
Surviving Redundancy
Working as a Holiday Rep
Working in Hotels & Catering
Working in Japan
Working in Photography
Working on Contract Worldwide
Working on Cruise Ships
Working with Children
Working with Horses

Other titles in preparation

The How To Series now contains more than 200 titles in the following categories:

Business Basics
Family Reference
Jobs & Careers
Living & Working Abroad
Mind & Body

Media Skills
New Technology
Student Handbooks
Successful Writing
Travel

Please send for a free copy of the latest catalogue for full details (see back cover for address).

JOBS & CAREERS

GETTING THAT JOB

How to make a success
of your job application

Joan Fletcher

4th edition

WHY DID YOU LIE
ON YOUR FORM?

I WANTED TO SHOW
THAT I WAS SOMEONE
WITH IMAGINATION!

How To Books

Cartoons by Mike Flanagan

British Library Cataloguing in Publication Data
A catalogue record for this book is available from the British Library.

Published by How To Books Ltd, 3 Newtec Place,
Magdalen Road, Oxford OX4 1RE, United Kingdom.
Tel: (01865) 793806. Fax: (01865) 248780.

First published 1987
Second edition 1991
Third edition 1993
Fourth edition (revised and updated) 1997

Note: The material contained in this book is set out in good faith for general
guidance and no liability can be accepted for loss or expense incurred as a result of
relying in particular circumstances on statements made in the book. The laws and
regulations are complex and liable to change, and readers should check the current
position with the relevant authorities before making personal arrangements.

Produced for How To Books by Deer Park Productions.
Typeset by Anneset, Weston-super-Mare, Somerset.
Printed and bound by Cromwell Press, Broughton Gifford, Melksham,
Wiltshire.

Contents

List of Illustrations

Preface

In today's society, there are often too many young people chasing too few jobs and the competition is fierce. Consequently, you may think 'What's the point in looking for a job – whenever there *is* a vacancy it is "snapped up" by somebody with better qualifications than I've got'. Well, if you *do* sit back and wait for something to come up, you may have to wait a long time for Lady Luck to smile on you. Buying this book shows you really want to work, so why not read on and find out how to make the most of yourself and take advantage of the opportunity to improve your chances of getting that job.

This book aims at helping all school-leavers as well as young people in their late teens and early twenties to get full-time employment. It should also help those young people who have been in jobs but, for some reason or other, have suddenly found themselves unemployed.

GETTING THAT INTERVIEW

The overall objective is to help you get an interview, then the job! You should find the comments helpful and informative in an up-to-date way, so that you can quickly adopt the most appropriate approach and know what services are available to help you achieve your objective. If you take the advice and develop the described skills associated with getting a job, then your efforts are more likely to be rewarded.

The contents emphasise the importance of preparing a plan of action, getting organised and knowing your job search area – whether in this country or abroad. (If you organise yourself, you stand more chance of being successful!)

SERVICES FOR JOB-HUNTERS

There is reference to the numerous services provided for young people – counselling facilities and opportunities for training within different types of training schemes. (You need to know what is available so you can take advantage of the situation and make the most of it!)

TECHNIQUES

Special techniques necessary for getting an interview, then the job, are described so that you can improve your communication skills – writing letters, completing application forms, expressing yourself either by telephone or in face-to-face situations. (The extent to which you will be successful in first, getting an interview and secondly, getting a job depends on how effectively you communicate!)

The contents also reflect that an employment interview is not a 'one off' situation, particularly in a business environment with (sometimes rapidly) changing technology and subsequent redundancies. Advice is given concerning the need to follow up the employment interview in a positive way by keeping contact with employment sources and developing your own job search programme, at the same time improving your communication skills.

CHECKLISTS

You will notice that at the end of most chapters there is a checklist which should help you organise your efforts and make it easy for you to see where you are going and what needs doing to get the best results.

There is also a list of useful addresses, together with a Further Reading section listing books and leaflets which might be of help to you in your job search.

If you follow the advice given in this book and make the most of every opportunity, you should be able to present yourself in the most favourable light and stand more chance of getting that job!

Joan Fletcher

1
Getting Organised

HAVING A POSITIVE ATTITUDE

Getting the right job is one of the most important things in your life
– and your parents' lives! Although luck can be an important factor,
you need to improve your chances by taking the initiative and adopt-
ing a positive approach towards finding a job. The alternative is to
wait for the right vacancy to come along, but if you do this the
chances of getting that job are limited.

Make the most of every opportunity; take advantage of the help
which is now available to young people. Of course, there are some
things you have no control over, such as the employment situation,
other applicants and interviewers. You may have had a job and been
made redundant. Even so, the fact that there are thousands of unemployed people does not necessarily mean that you don't stand an
earthly chance of getting a job. What it should do is emphasise the
importance of organising your efforts and working out the best and
most methodical way to get that job!

KNOWING THE LOCAL EMPLOYMENT SITUATION

Where you live determines employment prospects and usually the
best place to start is home. You can do casual jobs for the family and
neighbours, a part-time Saturday job. Show you *want* to work! If you
do a good job, then it increases your pocket money, enhances your
reputation in the community and enables you to acquire valuable
experience – an advantage at any employment interview. Meanwhile
you can find out what employment is available by 'keeping your ears
pinned back', *regularly* reading the adverts in the local newspapers,
visiting your Jobcentre, contacting your Careers Adviser and even
considering advertising your 'labour'.

Advertising yourself
This method is useful if your job area is far away from home and/or

you   have some special qualities or skills which are likely to be wanted by an employer. An example of this would be where you had good part-time experience in grooming and exercising horses or working on a farm during weekends and holidays and you wanted a full-time job doing such work. Another occasion when you might need to advertise your labour would be if you wanted a special type of practical, part-time work which would fit in with your educational studies at college or university.

GETTING INFORMATION

Listening to local radio

Your local radio station may be a useful source of information, particularly if there is a **Job Line** programme which regularly gives details of vacancies, including part-time and seasonal work in your area.

The **Help Line** is another useful feature of most local radio networks. These programmes are usually well organised/planned, so that they are presented in the best possible way and good advice is available from experienced people. Most of them are backed up by informative leaflets which you can get by writing to your local radio station.

'News and Views' programmes

The 'News and Views' programmes should help you get to know your area as they are related to current situations. If you listen to these regularly, you should find some of them particularly helpful and time-saving in your job search. Should you wish to widen your area and improve your knowledge of the national job situation, you can listen to national programmes which are directly about employment of young people. During the present state of high unemployment, you can expect several programmes to relate to your situation. A programme which will add to your knowledge of up-to-date national policies and practice is **File on 4** (Radio 4). As these national programmes have to be planned well in advance, you should to able to find out which are the relevant ones for you to listen to by writing to the BBC. However, if you want to plan on a weekly basis, then buy the *Radio Times* and *What's On TV* for details of the following week's radio and TV programmes with additional features, letters and information about current major issues.

Using television programmes

There are some television programmes which may help you in your job search. For instance, a series called **16 UP** includes issues such as job search and interviewing. You need to find out in advance about such series and also documentaries and **Action Line** programmes which will be relevant to your job search.

You may live in an area which presents a special 'Help Line' programme such as *This is Your Right* (Granada), in which case you can write to your local television centre for advice and relevant leaflets. This programme is particularly helpful because it also caters for deaf people by having someone communicate in sign language. There are also educational programmes, mainly on BBC2, and although some of these are linked with the Open University, you could improve skills such as conversational French/German/Spanish just by watching and listening. Occasionally there is a programme such as *Going to Work: Life and Social Skills* which you would find helpful. Also there are some useful 'News and Views' programmes for ethnic groups, such as *Asian Magazine* and *Gharbar*.

Broadcasting publications

If you write to the **BBC's Education Service**, they will advise you and give details of their comprehensive range of BBC publications: leaflets, books, tapes and videotapes. The other sources of information about radio and television programmes are the *Radio Times* and *What's on TV*.

USING YOUR LIBRARY

If you are unemployed and have time to spare, why not visit your local library and make use of the many facilities provided to help you in your job search? Don't be put off if your library is a modern one, using new information technology such as **computer** and **microfiche** systems. You only need to ask the librarian, who will advise you, so that part of your job search is made easier and quicker. Whatever your local library is like, there will be informative **leaflets** on display, usually presented in an eye-catching way. These are for quick reference but can also, if you choose, be taken away to read at leisure or refer to at a future date.

If you want to keep up to date with local information, there is a **noticeboard** which includes information sheets about educational, training and leisure activities. There may also be relevant forms for you to take away, complete and return to the organisation concerned.

NOTTINGHAM FIRE BRIGADE

PART-TIME

FIREFIGHTERS

Can you reach Smithtown Fire Station in less than four minutes? If so and you are well built, physically fit and aged 18–45 years, (male or female) we may be able to offer you a challenging part-time job as a retained firefighter. An annual retaining fee is payable as well as payment for responding to an incident and attending weekly training sessions. If you are a shift worker or self-employed and would be available during the day this would be an advantage.

If interested please contact the Officer in Charge on Smithtown 12345 during Office hours to arrange an appointment.

An Equal Opportunity Employer

PAPERBOYS-GIRLS required for news deliveries in the Smithtown area. Cycle essential. Good rates of pay for reliable people. – Please phone Mr Jones (91) 12345

EMPLOYMENT WANTED

ELECTRICIAN Anything considered. For a free quotation – Phone Smithtown 12345 (Mr Clark)
PLEASANT RELIABLE young lady 19, some experience, requires shop work. Presently working hence – Box Number X123 Smithtown Evening Post, Smith Street, Smithtown.
RETIRED ACTIVE LADY available for home duties. Cooking, caring etc – Tel: 12345
YOUNG MAN (22) with 6 years engineering experience including 2 years CNC operations and Basic programming seeks employment with company willing to offer further training in programming techniques. – Please reply to Box X124 Smithtown Evening Post, Smith Street, Smithtown.
YOUNG MAN 23, seeks employment. Experience in pricing contracts in the scrap industry. (Mainly railtrack.) Very reliable and quick to learn. Full driving licence. Absolutely anything considered. – Please phone Mr Jones on Smithtown 12345.
YOUNG LADY SEEKS Employment in cleaning work, experience in private houses – Ring 12345.
YOUNG GRADUATE mechanical engineer seeks employment. Phone Smithtown 12345.

WHY NOT CONSIDER?

PART-TIME WORK ...

... POSSIBLY LEADING TO A CAREER

SOUTHERN HUSSARS (TA) require fit, keen men to train as artillery observers, gunners, signallers, cooks and drivers. Aged 17–35 years – Please call for details at the TA Centre, Smith Lane, Blankly, Smithtown, between 10am and 4pm Sunday 6th April. Telephone 12345.

VOLUNTARY

EVER THOUGHT OF CONSERVATION? Why not join Blankly Valley Conservation Volunteers and learn new skills such as hedge laying, drystone walling, footpath construction and coppicing. We are a friendly group of people and work on a variety of sites throughout Smithshire. If you would like to join us on any day then ring us on – Smithtown 12345 or Blankly 3316.

ADVERTISING YOUR LABOUR

Fig. 1.   Exploring the possibilities.

In your job search many of the books you need to refer to are in the Reference Section, which means you will have to use them in the library. (Don't forget to take paper and pen to note the names and addresses!) The Reference Section also includes local and regional telephone directories as well as a selection of local and national newspapers. Main libraries usually have foreign newspapers as well as some business journals such as *The Caterer* which include local job vacancies.

It may be worthwhile to consider using the library on a more long-term basis, either to improve existing skills such as letter writing or to learn about new techniques. If so, you should consult the librarian, who will help you make the best use of the library's facilities.

CHECKLIST

1. Adopt a positive approach to jobhunting:
   - organise your efforts
   - try not to be disheartened if there are not many full-time jobs about.

2. Do casual work for family and friends.

3. Get a Saturday job or part-time work.

4. Show you *want* work!

5. Regularly read advertisements in local newspapers.

6. Visit your Jobcentre:
   - plan to be quick off the mark
   - follow up vacancies.

7. Consult your Careers Adviser: establish contacts.

8. Consider advertising yourself (your 'labour').

9. Listen to selected radio programmes: those which will help you in your job search.

10. Find out in advance which TV programmes will help you in your job search.

11. Make best use of your library's facilities to help you in your job search.

2
Knowing Your Job Search Area

KNOWING THE LOCAL WORK OPPORTUNITIES

You need to have a clear idea of the locality and work opportunities in relation to where you live. Obviously if an employer has a choice between you and someone who lives nearer the job, he/she would probably favour that person and your application could be pushed to the bottom of the pile.

If you live in a **rural area**, the opportunities for work are likely to be restricted, *eg* seasonal farm work, depending on what kind of business organisations there are. There might be a garden centre or, even better, a large company may have taken over a country mansion as its Training Centre, but in either instance there are not likely to be many full-time jobs for local young people. Generally, if you want a skilled full-time job, you will have to get away from your village and search in town or city.

Nowadays there are signposted **industrial estates**, usually to be found on the outskirts of towns and cities. Such concentrated areas of business organisations make it easier and worthwhile for you to call at their premises. If you intend to do this, it is advisable to buy a map of your locality and find out from your Council offices, library or Jobcentre where the companies are located.

There are some types of work which are always associated with certain areas. For instance, popular **tourist areas** are good sources of employment if you are interested in a job in catering or hotels. You can either contact individual hotels (listed in AA and RAC handbooks and Tourist Board information), or groups of hotels such as Trust Houses Forte. Perhaps the best contact would be an agency, especially if you are over 18 years old, with experience and/or skills to offer. In particular, specialist agencies are likely to have comprehensive information about employment conditions, such as accommodation provided. Most of these types of vacancies are for a season, usually the summer.

TRAVELLING TO AND FROM WORK

An employer realises that if you have to spend a lot of money in travelling to and from work, then you will tend to get disheartened and look for work nearer to home. Nowadays, as the cost of travel is of prime importance, you will have to consider several options. Would you walk, cycle, go by bus or train? Would you need to make special arrangements such as getting a lift from a friend or neighbour? Might you have to consider learning to drive; getting your own 'wheels' – scooter, motorbike, car?

Walking to work

Walk for regular exercise, to keep fit or because you enjoy walking. However, remember that your shoes will wear out quickly. Repairing or replacing them could be quite costly; also you'll need waterproofs to keep out the rain and snow!

Cycling to work

Cycle if you want the exercise and to go places the cheap way (once you have the bike). In some areas, this is pleasant and popular transport, an enjoyable way of getting to and from work. Too bad, though, if your cycle route is part of a busy road where you can't escape exhaust fumes and where cycling may be hazardous! Consider the cost of protective outer garments for bad weather; perhaps a need to carry, in a waterproof container, a change of outer clothes for use when you get to work.

Using your scooter, motorbike or car to get to work

If you are lucky enough to have your own 'wheels', you'll surely want to use them. You'll be transported to work in a flow of pride and pleasure! The bad news includes: cost and time involved in learning to drive; getting your vehicle, getting it on the road, keeping it there; (for scooter and motorbike) buying appropriate protective clothing, including essential safety helmet.
Tax, insurance and **service charges** eat up your money!

Getting a regular lift from friend or neighbour

If this is necessary, you will have to sort out certain things beforehand with the person concerned. For instance, are you going to pay a fixed sum of money each week or will you share costs? How much will this be in proportion to your weekly take-home pay? How reliable will the lift be? What happens if he/she is ill, or you can't get the lift for some other reason (*eg* car breakdown)? Is there a standby or alternative – what other arrangements do you need to make? Are there likely to be any snags? What about insurance cover and liability in case of accident?

Using public transport
Go by **bus** if the service is regular and convenient. It might be less costly if there are any **concessions** or special schemes for which you can be considered. Remember this is a changing scene. As a result of government policy, most areas now depend on privately operated buses, and scheduled services are often changed. If you live in the country, hard luck! The current, usually poor services, organised for shoppers rather than workers, are disappearing.

Go by **rail** if you live in an area where there are good commuter services. In some parts of the country, travel by rail is the best way of getting to work because it is quicker, more convenient, less 'hassle' and possibly cheaper (there are special schemes, such as **season tickets**).

Checklist for travel options
- *Cost* – how much per day/week/month?
- *Distance* – how far there and back each day?
- *Time* – when will you have to leave home?
- *Weather conditions* – will these affect your choice?
- *Independence* – will you need help to get to work?
- *Reliability* – can you be sure of being punctual?
- *Commuting* – can you save money?
- *Workmates* – do you want to travel with workmates?
- *Convenience* – how convenient will it be?
- *Choices* – have you considered all your options?

KNOWING YOUR LOCAL EMPLOYERS AND POTENTIAL EMPLOYERS

You need to start by finding out from your Jobcentre which organisations in your area regularly take on young people. For instance, most large international companies have a recruitment programme and on certain dates interested school-leavers are invited to apply, complete selection tests and be interviewed for only a few vacancies. Such companies may not take on many young people but they regularly recruit a few at certain times of the year.

If you are interested in a trade which involves you completing an

apprenticeship, you need to apply to the employer as early as possible because there is usually keen competition for few places. Your Careers Adviser and/or Jobcentre is likely to have a list of employers who offer apprenticeships. You could also apply personally to small businesses, such as electrical contractors, plumbers, *etc.*

You might find there are some local employers who have a feeling of **social commitment** to the community and, even in tough economic times, they let it be known that if possible they will employ young people. In your job search area there are also bound to be some employers who take on young people because it is cheaper to do so!

See how well you know *your* local employers:

1. Which is the biggest firm within 15 miles?
2. What kind of jobs does it offer?
3. Which are the 10 biggest office firms?
4. Which are the 10 biggest factories?
5. What local authority employers are there?
6. Which is the biggest hospital?
7. Which is the biggest hotel?
8. Which is the biggest engineering company?
9. How do you get to the nearest Jobcentre?
10. Which companies have announced expansion schemes?
11. Which have announced redundancies?
12. Which firm would you most like to work for?
13. Is there an industrial estate?
14. Is there a Chamber of Commerce? (It would probably issue a list of member firms.)

Fig. 2. Knowing your local employers.

Many companies, of different sizes, are prepared to employ young people on **training schemes**. If you are interested, it should help you to find out which of these companies tend to offer better training. It is surprising how much information you can acquire by observing, listening and asking such questions as 'Where is the training done?' 'How long does it take to become a skilled ... ?' Organised companies with proper, formal training schemes usually publicise the fact with informative leaflets which explain in detail what is involved, how long the training will take and what skills you finish up with.

If you want to know your job search area, you should try to find out as much as you can about the potential employers. (See also

Figure 2.) If you do this and use the information to your advantage as advised in Chapter 12, then you are more likely to be successful in not only getting that job but getting the right job.

CHECKLIST

1. Decide on your job search area – is it far from home?

2. If you are looking for a special type of work (*eg* hotel work), contact an agency.

3. Find out if any employer tends regularly to take on young people.

4. If you are interested in an apprenticeship, apply early.

5. Which employers have a good reputation for thorough training?

6. Get a map and details of companies involved before calling at business premises.

7. Check your travel arrangements. Any problems?

8. Know your travel cost so that you can relate it to take-home pay.

3
Careers Guidance and Counselling

CAREERS GUIDANCE AT SCHOOL: THE CAREERS TEACHER

Careers teachers in schools organise a wide programme of activities to help students prepare for leaving school. There are **visits** to colleges of further education, factories and offices; also **representatives** from these organisations visit schools and talk about work opportunities to groups of students.

The **careers teacher** is the link with other local education careers counselling sources (careers advisers, careers teachers in colleges) as well as employers in the community. You should discuss your career individually with your careers teacher at the earliest opportunity. Remember that he/she then knows you personally and information gained from the discussion should help future counselling sessions. It also enables you to make early contacts with people who can give you careers advice and gets you thinking about the issues that you will have to decide upon when leaving school.

CAREERS GUIDANCE AT A COLLEGE OF FURTHER EDUCATION

The careers teacher in a college does a similar job to the one at school. However, the extent of careers guidance varies considerably throughout the different colleges. In an active college, **careers counselling** operates on a systematic basis and is closely related to educational development programmes. Therefore you need to find out what careers counselling services are actually available at your college. If there is a leaflet explaining these services, fine! If there isn't, you should contact your careers teacher and find out the college procedure. The college library usually has relevant leaflets and is a good place to go with queries about careers information.

CHECKLIST

- How soon could you speak to your careers teacher?
- Where can you pick up any useful leaflets?
- What careers services are available to *you*?
- Is there more than one careers staff member?
- Have you checked the library for information?

---

1. **School achievements**
   Exams passed, subjects, grades
   Special achievements (*eg* swimming certificates)
   Responsibilities – prefect, Sports Captain, *etc*.
   Copy of school report (if you have a particularly good one, it is worth getting several copies, for possible employers).

2. **Personal strengths**
   Strong points, such as good attendance, reliability
   Responsibilities outside school (*eg* voluntary work, shopping for old people).

3. **Work experience**
   Any part-time jobs where you have worked during holidays or weekends – paper rounds, babysitting, fruit/vegetable picking, community work, *etc*.

4. **Interests**
   Even if you think there's nothing special about your interests, it is worthwhile considering in what way they may help *you* to decide the type of job for which you may be suited and the sort of organisation you would fit into.
   Examples: CB radio reflects practical person with more than general interest, possible for apprenticeship, training in electronics); helps parents with DIY jobs.

Fig. 3. Personal record for school-leavers.

YOUR CAREERS ADVISER

Your local **careers adviser** is a most important link between education and employment. At best he or she will give you careers advice so that there is more chance of (a) finding a job and (b) staying in that job because you are suited to it. You might live in a place where most local employers will not interview school-leavers unless arrangements have been made through the careers adviser. When this happens, it is the careers adviser, and possibly the careers, teacher, who does some **pre-selection**.

Whatever your situation, you need to be realistic. Try to remember that when the careers adviser interviews you, you are one out of hundreds of young people competing for a few jobs or further training. Often the careers adviser doesn't have much time to interview you and will rely on your school report. Therefore it is essential you provide a copy of this, together with a prepared **CV** (curriculum vitae, see Chapter 7) including interests and two names and addresses for **references**. You should be prepared to discuss your strong points. Make sure you don't lose your copy of the completed careers interview form, a useful document to be used for discussion with other careers counsellors. If you need further training the careers adviser can advise and make arrangements for you to go on a training scheme. Remember:

* be realistic

* organise yourself in advance

* get a copy of your school report

* have your CV ready

* keep your own copy of the careers interview form

* be fully prepared, and make the most of this important opportunity.

USING PRIVATE VOCATIONAL GUIDANCE AGENCIES

Whilst discussing your career with parents and/or relatives and friends, you may consider the possibility of using a private vocational guidance agency. Some of these organisations are well established and recognised by educational authorities; others advertise nationally in papers such as *The Independent* at appropriate times (*eg* summer holiday period). Most organisations are located in southern England, in

or near London. There are a few others in some cities but these tend
to specialise in a particular aspect of careers counselling, *eg* CV writers. Many of the national organisations deal with students who fail
their GCSE or A-levels.

Such an organisation would give you comprehensive vocational
guidance sometimes for a large fee. You would be expected to complete vocational aptitude tests and searching interviews. You need
not take the advice but at least you finish up knowing more about
your potential and can consider all aspects of further education and
training.

GETTING HELP FROM PARENTS, RELATIVES AND FRIENDS

Whatever your circumstances, it is always worth considering the views
of your parents, relatives and friends because usually they know you
for what you are and love you for your weaknesses as well as your
strengths. Although their opinions may conflict with yours, their
knowledge, experience and contacts could be very helpful.

CHECKLIST

1. If you are at school or college, see your careers teacher at the earliest opportunity.

2. If you are at college, find out about the college's careers counselling procedure.

3. Visit your library, and consult the librarian about careers information in books, *etc*.

4. See your local careers adviser and take with you your CV, a copy
   of your school/college report and written, up-to-date personal
   details (see Figure 3).

5. Discuss your career with your parents (and possibly certain rela-
   tives/friends).

6. Consider getting careers counselling from a private vocational
   guidance agency. (Remember you'll have to pay for this!)

4
Using Employment and Training Services

MAKING THE MOST OF GOVERNMENT SERVICES

During the last decade employment and training have been considerably influenced by changing conditions of employment and improved information technology. Today's high unemployment means
that you have really got to find out what kind of help is available
from the government's new schemes. When visiting a main employment office, you may be impressed by the modern technology with
busy staff dealing with (sometimes queues of) 'customers'. You will
find a wealth of **information** on display; masses of explanatory **leaflets**
(some quite colourful and appealing) all about:

- numerous training activities
- courses
- skills
- employment details
- vacancies
- job search advice.

However, you may not be so lucky in your part of the country.
Perhaps your Jobcentre does not seem to have all these facilities, or
maybe the helpful advice and support is less than you expected. If
so, it is worthwhile finding out which is the main employment office
in your area by looking in your local telephone directory. If you fully
explore all the facilities, you will realise how important a role the
Jobcentre plays in your life when you are one of several thousand
unemployed young people.

Of course, if your Jobcentre *is* well organised, with easily accessi-
ble information and supportive staff who discuss and advise in a most
helpful way, then it is *up to you* to make the best possible use of their
services!

VISITING THE JOBCENTRE

When you visit a Jobcentre, you need to know up-to-date details of:

* job vacancies
* whom to contact
* what to do so that you may be considered for the respective job.

If your Jobcentre gets news of vacancies and quickly displays them, then you can get speedily into action, there is no delay and you get a better chance of being considered for the job. After all, it may be a case of first come, first served!

How helpful are the Jobcentre services?

So that information on jobs can be quickly available, Jobcentre staff will try to maintain fairly close contact with local employers, to whom they can offer free services such as interview facilities and advice on employment problems. From your point of view, the extent to which this contact operates successfully will depend on how helpful the services are. For instance, you will not be impressed if you visit the Jobcentre each day and see the same adverts – no change. If you receive a telephone call requesting you to attend interview, you may take a dim view of the fact that 20 other people have also been directed by the same staff to attend! What might you think if you found that particular job was filled three days ago?

If you *do* have an unfortunate experience with one of the Jobcentres, don't let it put you off. Whatever the circumstances are, the facilities are there for you to make the best use you can of them. When everything and everybody works well, the whole setup goes with a zing! If the Jobcentre staff do their work by putting suitable people in touch with prospective employers, local companies are more likely to co-operate. The system works, there is a smooth flow of communication and everyone is happy – particularly *you* if you get the job!

USING A JOBCLUB

If you live in an area of high unemployment, you may find that there is a Jobclub. This exists to provide a place for people who have been unemployed for at least six months to get together to work at finding a job. The Jobcentre controls things and a member of its staff acts as leader and counsellor. There are usually about 20 members at any one time and the aim is to get each member fixed up with an appropriate job in the shortest possible time. Members stay on as long as it takes to get a job and they have to commit themselves to attending every session (at least four mornings each week).

Do you know:

• The address of the Jobclub nearest to your home?

• Its telephone number?

• The name of the organiser?

• The opening hours?

• How many members it has?

• Whether you know any members yourself?

• Whether the Jobclub produces an information leaflet you could get?

• Whether it can put you in touch with *other* Jobclubs in other localities?

• The times when it meets?

• What activities it offers?

• Whether you qualify to join?

The Jobclub leader shows members the best way to **contact employers** and make **job applications**. If you joined the Jobclub, you would be expected to carry out the advice given by using the facilities provided and contacting employers to apply for jobs. It is important to realise that all the resources, including telephone, paper, pen, envelopes, stamps and use of photocopier are **Free**!

If you are interested, contact your Jobcentre organiser who will make the necessary arrangements for you to join. However, do not be downhearted if you have to wait a while.

FINDING OUT ABOUT TRAINING

This is the area which changes according to employment needs and current government policy about the whole aspect of people at work and the country at work. Sometimes the name of a particular course will change, even though the associated skills are the same.

Sometimes the government will identify a particular national problem and inject £X million into a special project such as, recently, youth training. In that case, new types of courses emerge, so it is important for you to be aware of this possibility.

Lack of experience
When an employer says 'I'm really looking for someone with a bit more experience' it must be frustrating if you happen to have left school several months ago, applied for dozens of jobs and not been considered, even though the vacancies have been for a 16–18-year-old. Well, if you can't get a job to get the experience, you can have a go at acquiring skills of some sort.

Don't know what work you'd like?
You may not have much idea of the kind of work for which you might be suitable, or you may fancy what appear to you to be entirely different types of jobs (outdoors or in a shop). Then again, your ideas may keep changing because of what other people have said to you. You know the sort of remark: 'Why don't you go in for a steady trade like a plumber – you'll always be in work.' Or someone desperate to be helpful (often one of your parents) says, 'I can get you an interview at our place – it's quite good work really.' Good advice, but what really matters is that you know what you might be capable of doing and what kind of skills you can acquire in a planned way. Otherwise you could be running round in circles getting nowhere fast!

Getting advice and information
If you want to acquire new skills or improve those you have, you should see what the employment and training services can offer you. Not only can you find out about the different courses but experienced staff will give you an in-depth **interview** and advise what is most appropriate for YOU. You will be able to get free, up-to-date advice and information about any aspect of your career development and job search.

GAINING FROM SKILLS TRAINING

Skillcentres were originally set up throughout Britain by the government to provide intensive skills training. They now operate as private agencies along with other training providers, authorised by the local Training and Enterprise Councils (TECs). This has resulted in a more flexible approach to training. At the same time, people receive financial help from the government in the form of training allowances, travel costs and other assistance.

Which skills would help you most?

❑ Office	❑ Carpentry	❑ Factory work
❑ Secretarial	❑ Plumbing	❑ Community caring
❑ Book-keeping	❑ Electrical	❑ Vehicle servicing
❑ General catering	❑ Plastering	❑ Electronics
❑ Bakery	❑ Computer	❑ Other
❑ Food service	❑ Data processing	
❑ General building	❑ Business studies	

Getting information
The number of Skillcentres and the training skills involved differ according to the area and job opportunities. You will be able to find names and addresses in your local telephone directory but if you wish for more information it is advisable to contact your careers adviser or Jobcentre.

Making arrangements for training
When you agree to complete a specific course, your careers adviser will make the necessary arrangements with the Skillcentre concerned. During your training, you will be responsible to a **supervisor** in the same way you would in any formal work situation.

Recognising your achievement
At the end of the course, although you won't have the depth of skills and experience that you would on a complete apprenticeship scheme, you will achieve some skills and you may pass some educational examination. You will have done something constructive and any prospective employer will be able to see evidence of your training.

What would YOU gain from skills training?

- ❏ Work experience
- ❏ Having proper training
- ❏ Trying new skills
- ❏ Meeting new people
- ❏ Getting a qualification
- ❏ Practice in taking tests
- ❏ Learning to use new equipment
- ❏ Giving me something worthwhile to do
- ❏ Getting a reference for a future employer
- ❏ Helping me decide on a new career

WORKING FOR YOURSELF

If you are keen to work for yourself and have the ability, ideas and will to succeed, you should contact the **Prince's Youth Business Trust (PYBT)** – a charity which helps young people, aged 18–25 (or 18–30 for people with disabilities) to set up in business. It offers expert advice and financial help in the form of grant(s), and/or loan (with very reasonable repayments).

For further information see your local telephone directory or write to the Prince's Trust headquarters in London.

CHECKLIST

1. Know what facilities are available at your Jobcentre.

2. *Regularly* visit your Jobcentre – be aware of the job market.

3. Read details of job vacancies – know what job opportunities are available.

4. Find out about different training schemes by asking Employment Training staff and reading leaflets.

5. Ask for an in-depth interview and vocational guidance.

6. Act quickly on any information given to you by Employment Training services.

7. Do not keep changing your mind about what you want to do – be realistic and listen to advice given.

8. Let your Jobcentre know immediately if you go for interview and find the vacancy has been filled.

9. Be prepared for an employer to say, 'I am really looking for someone with more experience.' Try to convince him/her that you are worthy of being given a chance.

10. If you belong to a Jobclub, act quickly on advice given and make full use of these free facilities!

5
Getting onto Training Schemes

UNDERSTANDING THE PURPOSE OF TRAINING SCHEMES

You can formally acquire skills and get work experience by completing one or more of the several government-funded training schemes. As these are modified from time to time, you will need to keep your information up-to-date.

These schemes are planned to provide quality training related to job opportunities within the locality and at the same time emphasise the importance of continued education. Each Training and Enterprise Council (TEC), Careers Centre and Jobcentre plays an important part in ensuring that there is a flexible approach towards training, so labour skills match the demands of local employers.

Are you aged 16–18 years and leaving school or college?

If you have taken notice of your careers teacher and careers adviser, by the time you leave school or college you should have a pretty good idea of what action to take in order to get your first 'real' job. You might already have acquired experience – a paper round or weekend job. You may have completed a one-year or two-year BTEC course and obtained useful qualifications (National Vocational Qualifications). You might even get a job straight away, having worked towards this achievement whilst in your last year at school/college.

Using your experience and qualifications

When seeking your first job, you should find your work experience *and* qualifications at least get you an interview with a prospective employer. Of course, your work experience might lead to employment opportunities – through contacts, *etc.* – but it is more likely that it will help accelerate your formal training for a job, by getting accepted on a training scheme arranged by your careers adviser.

Gaining experience through training
Perhaps you have not had the opportunity to get work experience? Do not despair or lose interest. It is not too late to acquire formal work skills training and, hopefully, National Vocational Qualifications (NVQs). Your careers adviser will be able to help you and organise your Jobsearch plan.

Are you over 18 years and out of work?
If you are over 18 years and seeking a job, when you visit the Jobcentre to find out about vacancies, you should see an **Employment Training Adviser** about getting formal skills which will help you get a job. He/she will help you decide what might be the most suitable training for you, bearing in mind the current employment climate.

Maintaining and updating your skills
There is so much redundancy these days and an increasing number of companies going 'bust' that it is quite common for people over 18 years old suddenly to find themselves unemployed. If you have to face this situation you are likely to ask yourself whether you should update the skills you already have or get trained in new skills.

You may find yourself unemployed for a long time, so it will be important to maintain those skills, possibly improve them or train in new skills which might lead to better opportunities. Whichever you decide upon will improve your chances of getting a job, keep you in the habit of work and boost your morale!

THE RANGE OF TRAINING SCHEMES

Nowadays there are many types of training schemes available, ranging from **Basic Skills** (reading, writing, arithmetic as work-related skills) to **Modern Apprenticeships** (training schemes lasting 3–5 years, leading to high levels of skills and qualifications (NVQs) within sectors such as Information Technology and Retail as well as traditional industries – see Figure 4).

If you need to brush up your literacy and numeracy skills or if English is not your first language, **Basic Skills** can be included as part of your training programme.

Perhaps you feel you just want to **improve your interview techniques**, and also get help in preparing a CV and planning your jobsearch. In that case you will choose one of the short duration (3–5 days) training schemes.

After discussion with your Employment Training Adviser you may

DESIGNED TO GIVE YOU THE BEST START TO YOUR CAREER	Open Day 12 April

If you're looking for a high quality alternative to academic routes, which provides paid employment too, it's time to talk to INTEC.

Our students achieved the first two Modern Apprenticeships in Administration in the country, qualifications which gave them the equivalent of A-levels and paved the way towards university entrance – all achieved with the support of the employers.

With our expertise behind you, we'll get you started. BTEC & RSA, Accountancy to Marketing – there's a lot going on at INTEC.

For further details, an information pack, or to arrange an interview contact:

Pat Smith
INTEC BUSINESS COLLEGES
Barras House
1 Gold Street
Blankly BL1 5JJ
Tel: 8965 Fax: 1479

APPRENTICE ELECTRICIANS WANTED

The Electrical Contracting Industry can offer up to
60 MODERN APPRENTICESHIPS IN THE BLANKLY AREA IN 199X
If you are 16–18 years old and would like to know more about the industry and the opportunities available why not come along, with your parents if you wish, to the:

OPEN EVENING
for
ELECTRICAL INSTALLATION MODERN APPRENTICESHIPS
on
Tuesday 25 February
at
THE PEOPLE'S COLLEGE
SMITHSON WAY, BLANKLY
from
5.30pm to 7.30pm

Visit the Electrical Installation Workshops, meet S D Ltd, employers, current apprentices and see a presentation about career and training opportunities within the Electrical Contracting Industry.
For further information contact:
Sue Payne S D L Park Lane Works, Old Blankly.
Tel: 977 1471

AGED 16–23 and LOOKING FOR A CAREER?

EARN WHILE YOU LEARN!
MODERN APPRENTICE-SHIPS
in Business Administration
Information Technology
Retailing

Open the door to a job and a career with local employers. We have opportunities for immediate employment. Good standard of education and determination to succeed required.

For an immediate interview call Denise now 950 5777

BFD Training

Market Square House, St Peter Street, Blankly

Fig. 4. Advertisements for Modern Apprenticeships.

Fig. 4. Contd.

be interested in a **more comprehensive training scheme** which will result in your acquiring skills *and* work experience within your chosen area of employment. A job is not guaranteed, but completion of such a scheme will be a positive step towards employment. You will stand a better chance of employment if you are flexible about the type of work you do.

HAVING YOUR PERSONAL DETAILS READY

You need to be prepared for a lot of form filling, so make sure you have *all* your personal details and documents readily available when you attend your interview at the Jobcentre. This will be particularly important when you complete your Training Agreement or are discussing claims such as Jobseeker's Allowance.

TAPS (TRAINING ACCESS POINTS)

You will be able to take advantage of recent developments in computer technology and get quick access to wide-ranging information about education and training for all kinds of skills at every level. This TAPS service is available at your Jobcentre, Careers Office, library and possibly at other locations such as the Training Commission Area Office or Inner City Employment Office.

WORK IN THE COMMUNITY SCHEMES/PROJECTS

These are schemes for the unemployed, aged 18–59. They would interest you if you wanted to do temporary work that benefits the community. The work could involve conserving wildlife, renovating houses, helping charities, maintaining footpaths and helping run luncheon clubs for old people.

The duration of the project and type of work you would do would depend on what the purpose was. If you live in an area where the authorities have decided to fund a scheme involving clearing canals then that task would take a long time even if a large group of people were taking part. On the other hand, the project may be an ongoing community scheme such as running city farms or gardening and decorating for elderly and disabled people, in which case you might be accepted for short periods of employment.

Despite occasional adverse comments about this type of work (cheap labour, etc.) if you get involved you will benefit in several ways. For instance, it could be something that you have wanted to do, perhaps, for the good of the community (*eg* helping the elderly and disabled). It would keep you in the **habit of work** and you would make new friends and contacts. Your particular project may also enable you to get some useful formal training.

Do YOU want ...

- ❑ Something worth doing?
- ❑ To keep the work habit?
- ❑ To make new friends?
- ❑ To see new places?
- ❑ To try something new?

- ❑ To get a reference?
- ❑ To get experience?
- ❑ To keep fit and active?
- ❑ To hear about new jobs?

Then Work in the Community Schemes could be for you.

TRAINING COURSES FOR THOSE WITH SPECIAL NEEDS

If you are a **young disabled person**, training can be arranged at any time after leaving school. This could include the usual Youth Training where there is a certain flexibility concerning the time factor of when you have to do the training (*eg* you may be accepted for Youth Training up to the age of 21).

In addition, there are special training opportunities:

- *With an employer* who is prepared to train you and employ you for at least six months after the training has finished.
- *At a residential centre* which is staffed and equipped to cater for people with special needs. Consequently, a wide range of training such as computer programming is offered, depending upon the area of your interest.

The centre may be a small set-up with hostel accommodation provided, or you could attend one of the big residential centres such as St Loyes College for Training the Disabled for Commerce and Industry, Exeter, Devon, or the Royal Blind School, Edinburgh, where courses include shorthand-typing, audio-typing and switchboard operating.

Additionally, your local authority may be one of those which provide **educational grants** especially for disabled people to study for the professions. If you require information and advice, contact your **disability employment adviser** or, if you are under 19 years of age, your local careers adviser.

CHOOSING PRIVATE TRAINING

You, or you and your parents, may decide it will be best to acquire certain skills at a privately-run training centre. You could be the type of person who is more likely to benefit from personal, private tuition rather than by joining a group on a government training scheme. Whatever the reason, if you opt for private training, you must be prepared to pay for it.

In fact, when there is high unemployment, it may be well worth thinking about whether to spend money on intensive training in order to improve your chances of getting a job. After all, you should be successful if your private organisation has good contacts with employers. In addition, if your chosen private training company is well-known, then employers will be impressed by its reputation and consequently be more interested in your application.

CHECKLIST

1. Have personal details and dates available at your initial Employment Training interview.

2. Include your CV – as a basic fact sheet to help you *and* your Employment Training Adviser.

3. Be honest and realistic when discussing your training needs.

4. Listen carefully to your adviser – it should help you decide what your training needs are.

5. Be positive about your training programme and flexible in your choice of work.

6. Use the time to update and improve your skills.

7. Think about the benefits of acquiring new skills.

8. Be prepared to complete several forms including claims for benefit whilst seeking work. Have documents (certificates, references, *etc.*) readily available.

9. Ensure you fully understand what is involved before you commit yourself and sign any Employment Training Agreement.

10. If you lose interest in your training programme, discuss this immediately with your Employment Training Adviser. Remember your (signed) Training Agreement!

6
Responding to Advertised Vacancies

VISITING YOUR JOBCENTRE

It is important to visit your Jobcentre regularly – not just when you happen to be near one. You need to be aware of what jobs are available, not only for the moment but for future plans. For instance, you may be interested in a particular job but know that you need more qualifications and that makes you decide on a college course.

If you have a query, ask the Jobcentre staff, and ensure they know you are keen to get a job as quickly as possible. Don't worry that they may think you are a 'pain'. They are more likely to put you in touch with a job just to get rid of you!

The important thing is to know about *all* vacancies, bearing in mind that it may be necessary to acquire further education or training before you can be considered for the kind of job you would like to do.

VACANCIES ADVERTISED ON TELEVISION AND LOCAL RADIO

Some television companies and local radio stations have regular (Jobwatch/Jobfinder) programmes which feature a selection of vacancies – most of the information being provided by the local Jobcentre. It would be worthwhile finding out about such programmes.

UNDERSTANDING ADVERTISEMENTS

Most employers like to be selective and advertise a vacancy so that they have as wide a choice as possible (it is quite common to have two or three hundred replies to a block advert).

Adverts for young people vary in size and content. Generally, block adverts are informative, reflecting what the job involves, qualifications and skills required, training, *etc*. Other personal requirements may be stated: 'must be smart in appearance' ... 'have a good personality'. You should also look for the small advert which gives only brief details. It is worthwhile following this up because there may well be a super job in it for you!

Figure 5 contains examples of typical advertisements. Think about how you would apply for one of those jobs.

RELYING ON HEARSAY – FRIENDS, RELATIVES

In many places, usually small communities, informal communication has considerable influence regarding job prospects. Word gets passed around that there may be a job going at ... Frequently, jobs are 'found' as a result of chat over a glass of beer or a cup of coffee, although perhaps it isn't as easy for that to happen these days because of the tough economic situation.

There are also still some organisations which, as a matter of company policy, advertise within the company first, in order to encourage friends and relatives to apply.

You should quickly follow up any hearsay, but remember that there may *not* be a job or possibly there *is* a job but you are not suitable. The main thing is to keep trying and one day you may be lucky!

Which of these have *you* tried?

- Asking all your family and relatives?
- Asking your neighbours?
- Asking your own friends and acquaintances?
- Asking school or college friends?
- Asking teachers and lecturers you know?
- Asking any business people you know?
- Asking at any clubs you belong to?
- Writing to anyone?
- Asking any other friends in work?

USING EDUCATIONAL SOURCES – SCHOOL, COLLEGE, CAREERS ADVISER

If you live in an area where the careers guidance services are most active, there will be strong **links with local employers**. At school, employers or their representatives will talk to groups of students about opportunities in their organisations and interviews will be arranged. At your college of further education, there is likely to be much closer liaison with employers.

When careers teachers are informed of vacancies, they will pass the

CLERICAL

YOUNG PERSON
16–17 required to train as
RECEPTIONIST/CLERK
Male or Female
Must be very keen and willing to
learn.
TELEPHONE 12345

YOUNG PERSON required to operate new work control system in busy photocopying servicing department in Blankly. Must have good telephone manner and be able to record messages accurately, to receive incoming service calls and allocate calls to engineers as well as general office duties. A knowledge of the surrounding area would be an advantage. – Please telephone 12345 for an application form.

16–17 YEAR OLD. Well spoken and with minimum 4 GCSEs, including Maths and English, is required for reception and general office duties – Written applications including CVs to Jones & Jones, Chartered Accountants, 116 Smithville Road, Smithtown SM12 3XX. (No agencies.)

SECRETARIAL

ADMINISTRATOR required for company close to city centre. Position demands a confident outgoing person (male or female) with an excellent telephone manner and organisational skills. Salary negotiable. For further details contact – Janice Jones, Simon Smith Recruitment Consultants on 12345.
AN ADVANTAGE to be trained at Smithville Business College! Contact our qualified tutors and then decide. RSA-Pitman Centre, Secretarial–Computer courses Basic–Advanced. Flexi hours. 12345.
BLANKLEY TRAINING CENTRE Blankly House, 18 High Road. An RSA, Pitman, EMFEC Examination Centre. For professional courses in Teeline, Pitman 2000 and New Era Shorthand, Typewriting, Word Processing and Book-Keeping (Manual & Computerised Systems) – Tel: 12345.
A1 SHT AND AUDIO SECS urgently req. (male or female) for immd bookings. Top rates – Contact Smithline Agy, St. Peter's St., Smithtown. Tel 12345.
A1 TEL-REC'S req for immd assignments both in the centre and surrounding areas. Exp of Monarch, Kinsman and 4 × 18 flick adv. Top rates – Contact Smithline Agy, St. Peter's St., Smithtown. Tel 12345.

SCHOOL-LEAVER 16–17 yrs old required to train as Office Junior in a small office environment. Must be of pleasant disposition. WP experience advantageous. – Written application only including full CV to Jones Limited, Midtown Offset House, Victoria Avenue, Upper Smith Street, Blankly, Smithville XX1 1XX.

SECRETARIAL

SHORTHAND TYPIST

required by Jones Ltd for their head office situated on Smithville Road, Blankly.

Applications (male or female) aged 18 plus will have obtained speeds of 80 wpm shorthand and 40 wpm typing. Experience of word processing would be advantageous.

Please apply in writing to the
PERSONNEL MANAGER
JONES LIMITED
243 SMITHVILLE ROAD
BLANKLY
SMITHTOWN
XX1 1XX
Giving full details of age,
qualifications and experience

JOIN A WINNING TEAM

SALES OFFICE
ASSISTANT
Male or Female

Required to provide backup services to our Sales Liaison and Marketing Services division. typing/filing/sales statistics. Scope to work on own initiative. Word processing skills advantageous but not essential as training will be given. Previous office experience essential. Ideally aged 18–25 years.

Telephone Tony Smithson
SMITHTOWN 12345

THE SMITHTOWN CLUB

Exclusive City Centre Club

requires full-time day

RECEPTIONIST

He-she will be aged 21 years plus, with approximately 2–3 years experience in typing, switchboard work an advantage.

A pleasant personality and ability to deal with people essential. This is a demanding job which requires tact, efficiency and an ability to cope under pressure as well as a sense of humour.

Excellent references essential, good salary, 4 weeks holiday per annum, lunches provided.

Please apply in own handwriting giving full details of career to date enclosing a photograph.

Miss M. Jones, The Smithtown Club, 16–20 Smithville Road, Smithtown.

Fig. 5. Typical advertisements.

Fig. 5. Contd.

information on to the students, then arrange interviews and supply college references. Your local careers adviser provides the most important source of known vacancies for young people.

Who is my local careers adviser?

NAME _____

ADDRESS _____

_____

Tel: _____

If all these educational services work smoothly and efficiently, you could be one of many young people who get jobs for which they are likely to be most suited.

USING PRIVATE EMPLOYMENT AGENCIES

Most of these, particularly the national bureaux, are located in cities and large towns. Generally speaking, private agencies do not cater for young people, unless they have some special skill or experience to offer. Exceptions to this would be those agencies which deal with residential domestic work, including assistant nursery nursing, either in this country or abroad (if abroad, applicants must be over 18 years old). If you *do* have some skill or experience, it is always advisable to contact these private employment agencies in order to keep up to date with the employment situation. They may also put you in touch with part-time employment.

WORKING AT SEA

Some agencies located in port areas deal with applications for those wishing to **work at sea**. If you are interested in such a career, there are opportunities to become a trainee with a private shipping company or join the Merchant Navy. You don't need formal academic qualifications to be a deck rating, although GCSEs would be useful. However, if you wish to become an officer, you will need at least five GCSEs. When accepted, you will be able to progress through the officer grades by experience and successfully taking exams for higher grades.

Needless to say, if you wish to work at sea, good health and fitness are essential requirements. In addition, if you intend working in the general manning of a ship, you must have perfect colour vision without glasses or contact lenses.

WORKING IN THE SERVICES

If you like the idea of travel, training and good pay, all within a disciplined life, then you should consider joining one of Her Majesty's Services the Navy, Army or Air Force.

All three Services have Careers Information Offices located throughout the country and if you are considering such a career, you should write to the nearest one (address in your local telephone directory). You should bear in mind that there are not as many openings in the **Navy and Air Force**. You will need some GCSEs to support your application. In both these Services, there are different schemes of entry depending on your academic qualifications.

Generally, there are more opportunities in joining the **Army** and the different schemes of entry depend on your aptitude as well as age and qualifications (you don't need academic qualifications for some schemes of entry and will be accepted providing you pass certain aptitude tests, a thorough medical examination and interviews).

Young men 16–17$^1/_2$ years old

If you have a flair for **music**, you can apply to be a Junior Bandsman. As well as being taught to play an instrument, if you have exceptional musical talent, you could get a year's course at the Royal Military School of Music.

On the other hand, you might think you have **leadership qualities** and want the opportunity to develop those at an early age. If so, you should apply to be considered as a Junior Leader.

Perhaps you fancy being trained as a **technician or craftsman**? If so, you can apply for Junior entry as an apprentice technician or craftsman and be trained in two years at the Apprentice College.

If you are over 17 years old, with at least five GCSEs you could be considered for the School entry for **Regular Commissions**.

Young women over 17 years old

You can join any of the Services and be trained for one of a variety of jobs such as driving, clerical, technical *etc.*, *or* QARANC and be trained for one of a few non-nursing jobs, including clerical and laboratory technician work.

Applying and attending interview

If you are interested in any branch of the Services, you should write to the nearest Service Careers Information Office. You will be invited to attend interview, complete several selection tests and undergo a thorough medical examination. If successful and depending on your entry scheme, you will be required to sign on for a specified number of years, with an option to leave the Service after a certain time.

CHECKLIST

1. Visit your Jobcentre frequently.

2. Read local newspaper advertisements regularly.

3. Don't overlook the small adverts.

4. Study the adverts carefully. See what is needed: do you match up to job requirements?

5. Decide how to reply – letter, phone or call at business premises.

6. If you hear of a (possible) vacancy, follow up without delay.

7. When educational sources (school, college, careers adviser) publicise vacancies, follow up immediately.

8. If appropriate, consider using the services of private employment agencies.

9. Keep up to date with the employment situation; get to know the job market.

7
Writing Application Letters

MAKING AN IMPACT ON PAPER

Most employers ask you to apply in writing (see Figure 6). An employer will be influenced by what he/she *sees*, *ie* the **general appearance** of your letter of application:

- type of paper used
- layout and presentation
- legible writing
- balanced paragraphs

Then he/she will be further impressed upon reading the **contents**: is the meaning clear, with good sentence construction, correct spelling and appropriate punctuation? Is the information organised? Are the comments relevant? (Do you expect an employer to have either time or inclination to read irrelevant comments, however interesting they may be!) Avoid being too lengthy, at the same time ensuring that your comments reflect a clear overall impression of you in relation to the job. Aim to write a letter of application which has the qualities of a good business letter, yet is individualistic, revealing your strengths.

CHOOSING YOUR PAPER AND PEN

Avoid using lined paper, however tempting it may be to do so, especially if your handwriting is big and sprawly, or if you tend to write sloping instead of straight across the paper of unlined paper. An employer will favour good quality, unlined paper and often not bother to read lined paper. If you decide to use good quality coloured paper, please consider the reaction of the reader (perfumed, lilac-coloured paper from a young man may well be misinterpreted!).

It is also important to consider the type of pen you use as this will

JUNIOR LABORATORY ASSISTANT

Expansion of our laboratory facilities has given rise to a vacancy for a Junior Laboratory Assistant.

The work will mainly involve routine testing of paper and plastic products and associated raw materials. The ideal candidates will be aged 16–20 with GCSE or equivalent qualifications in maths, English and a scientific subject.

Please apply in writing, with full details to

**MISS A. B. SMITH
BLANKLEY PACKAGING CO. LIMITED
Road Six, Industrial Estate,
BLANKLEY, SMITHSHIRE**

OPPORTUNITY for young person to be trained in all aspects of greengrocery trade. Aged 16–18 years. Must be reliable and of smart appearance. Apply in writing to Miss T Jones, The Fruit Shop, The Precinct,Blankley, Smithtown.

YOUNG PERSON

required to train as
DISPENSING
OPTICIAN
in Blankly

Must have 5 GCSEs or equivalent, including Maths and English language.

The successful candidate will have a pleasant personality and be of smart appearance.

Application in writing to Mr G Jones, Jones & Jones Limited, 25 Blankly Street, Smithtown.

SMITH LIMITED

Jewellers
**OFFER
TRAINEE POSITION
FOR 16-YEAR-OLD SCHOOL-LEAVER**

Applicants should have good level of Maths and English education and will be given full basic training into retail jewellery.

**Apply in writing only please to:
SMITH LIMITED
Blankly Road, Smithtown,
Smithshire**

UNITED BLANKLEY
INSURANCE PLC
TRAINEE AGENT

A position has arisen for a trainee agent working in the Smithshire area. This is a permanent pensionable position, age 17/20, English language and mathematics a requirement. Salary plus commission.

Apply in writing to Mr F. N. Jones, Branch Manager, United Blankley Ins. plc., 73 Smith Street, Smithtown.

Fig. 6. More examples of advertisements – asking you to reply in writing.

influence your writing. Obviously you will know which type of pen will produce your best, most legible writing.

PRESENTATION: ORGANISING YOUR CONTENTS

The reader will be influenced by the layout of your letter. Practise writing two or three examples, and check each one:

- Is it recognised business format?

- Is the message presented so that the reader will be interested in your application?

- Are the essential facts clearly and briefly presented so that the employer does not have to search for them.

Consider how much more can be communicated by implication and, if possible, include useful information which is relevant to job requirements and will add to the 'depth' of your profile. Your comments should clearly show that you have thought about and/or found out about what the job involves and that you possess certain qualities worthy of consideration. (See also Chapter 17.)

WRITING AN EXPLORATORY LETTER

If you live in an area where there are many developing firms or large organisations, this approach can be most successful (see Figure 7). You write this type of letter when there isn't a known vacancy but you would like to work for that particular company and believe you have something to offer. When there isn't a job, it is most important to make some impact relating to your strengths. Unless you prepare your letter carefully, you are likely to get the reply 'Thank you but . . . no vacancies'.

To get good impact, you need to present an organised, typed CV (**curriculum vitae**, see below) together with a handwritten letter, both preferably on one side of the paper only. The **handwritten letter** should have correct business letter layout with three or four paragraphs. It should be legible, brief and clear, with meaningful comments reflecting your strong points. Aim to tell a prospective employer about yourself at that time and imply possible development of your strong points so that you will be regarded as worthy of consideration for employment.

If you have been made redundant, do not be afraid to give details.

6 Pear Tree Drive
Balmuir
BK9 2AO

Dear Mr Johnson,   8th April 9X

Will you please consider me for a suitable vacancy within your organisation.

I am 18 yrs old and will be finishing a 2 yrs Business Studies (BTEC) National Diploma Course this June. During the course, I have been able to do part-time work, weekends and holidays, working for an Estate Agent — However, I do not wish to pursue that type of work for my career.

Working for your company appeals to me because you have a good reputation for giving young people the chance to prove themselves. Also, I know several of your employees.

I enclose my C.V. and meanwhile should be grateful if you would grant me an interview.

Yours sincerely,

James Pontin.

Mr C. Johnson.
General Manager
National Insurance
The Square
Balmuir   BK1

Fig. 7. Exploratory letter. When sent with a typed CV, this would have good impact. Comments are positive and brief. The writer knows about business format and the handwriting is legible.

Redundancy should never be concealed because this would only come out at an interview and the interviewer would suspect you of hiding something. The important thing is that you have acquired work experience and, possibly, skills.

PREPARING YOUR CURRICULUM VITAE (CV)

Your CV should be word-processed (or typed) in order to achieve the best possible impact. Unless you have word-processing or typing skills, it is advisable to get some help with this. Once you have produced a good, well-presented CV, make several photocopies of it – most useful if you have to write many letters of application.

You need to organise the details to make easy reading. Presentation is vitally important so that the reader can, at a glance, see essential 'blocks' of facts. These will cover personal details, education and qualifications, experience, interests and the names and addresses of two people who would give you references (see Figure 8). If your CV is well designed, it can also be a useful document for the employer to use during your interview.

Remember:

- The **typed** CV makes the best impression.

- Use the CV to **say as much as you can** about yourself.

- Use plenty of clear **headings**.

- Make plenty of good clear **copies** for future use.

- Always make sure it is **up to date**.

CHECKLIST

1. Your application letter should be as brief as possible, yet contain the information the employer requires (personal details related to the job).

2. It should be clearly written on good quality, unlined paper with correct business letter layout and presentation.

3. The letter may have an attached CV stating relevant details: name, date of birth, marital status, address, telephone number, driving licence, education and qualifications, work experience, interests, references.

Name: BURNSWELL Mary Joanne

27 Elmsworth Road
NEVERTON
Nr Derby
Date of birth: 21 Apr 8X   DE90 1LN

Marital status: Single   Tel: Neverton 93784

Provisional driving licence

EDUCATION AND QUALIFICATIONS

School	From	To			
Neverton Comprehensive	9X	9Y	6 GCSEs incl.	English Language French Maths Chemistry	Grade B B C D
			+ RSA	Typewriting	Stage 1

Further education

Lumley College   9X - 1 year full-time Business Studies course (BTEC)
              incl. Data Process; People & Communication

WORK EXPERIENCE

From	To	Employer	Job responsibilities
Sept. 9Z Hols & Sats	–	J Durmond & Co Engineering Derby	Typist/General Clerical Assistant Invoicing - customer queries Relief Switchboard Operator
9Y and 9Z Summer hols		Post Office/Store Neverton	Sales Assistant - helped with ordering and checking stock

INTERESTS

Home: cooking; helping mother; decorating; painting

Social: dancing; pop concerts;, belong to local Youth Club

Sports: particularly tennis; enjoy cycling; support Neverton United

REFERENCES

Mr L Smithson, General Manager   Ms V Hobson, Postmistress
J Durmond & Co   Neverton Post Office
Alton Road   NEVERTON
DERBY DE41 8VB   Nr Derby DE99 1LN

Tel: Derby 61034   Tel: Neverton 41096

Fig. 8. Example of curriculum vitae (CV).

4. The 'tone' of your letter should reflect your personal profile, emphasising your strengths related to the job. When there is no vacancy, it is particularly important to make some impact relating to your strengths.

5. Always read through what you have written to ensure it makes sense and is accurate, brief and clear!

8
Filling out Application Forms

WHY DO EMPLOYERS USE APPLICATION FORMS?

Many firms use some kind of application form to help them shortlist applicants for interview. The form can also be used as a source document (personal record) of the employee. A contract of employment is based upon the completed application form, so you can appreciate how important it is to both employer and employee.

Some large organisations have special forms for different groups of workers but generally an application form is designed for people of all ages with varying experience and qualifications. Bear this in mind when completing an application form and don't be 'put off' by questions which seem inappropriate to you.

UNDERSTANDING THE QUESTIONS

It is always necessary to read an application form carefully before you put pen to paper, so that you fully understand the questions. The company is not trying to catch you out by asking tricky questions, but there may be words that you don't understand. If necessary, use a dictionary to find out what the question is all about.

Use a spare sheet of paper or a photocopy of the form to jot down points *before* you actually write on the form (see Figure 9). In this way it will be possible to see how the information will look. Will it be clear and in logical order? It also gives you the opportunity to check that the information is accurate *before* you commit yourself to paper.

GIVING A GOOD IMPRESSION

Use the application form to help you present your best, true profile, with an accurate record of personal details, qualifications, skills and experience. Include redundancy details if applicable.

Make sure you include part-time work and write meaningful com-

Below are some questions which need to be considered carefully and your answers written down on separate paper before you complete the application form. Organise your answer – make sure comments are accurate, brief and clear!

Question: State interests and hobbies including positions of responsibility held.

Question: Give brief details of the hobbies, sports and societies which are most important to you. Mention any offices held and any awards or distinctions you have obtained.

Example answer: Stamp collecting for six years (most valuable stamp worth £35).
Just started to learn to drive.

Example answer: Reading – mostly historical novels; belong to local library.
Home – cook for family at weekends.
Outdoor – walking, cycling, some bird-watching (belong to RSPB).

Question: Write briefly about your career to date. Refer to your achievements and ambitions. Mention any aspect which you think is important in relation to this job.

Answer: (Your comments need to be accurate, brief and clear; in logical order so there is a good' flow' and the reader gets a better 'picture' of you and how you see yourself in this job. Relate your strong points, experience, *etc.* to the job requirements.)

Question: State any additional information you consider relevant to your application.

Answer: (Consider all questions (and information on CV) – do your answers reflect a complete profile, emphasising your strengths in relation to the job? If NO, then write down missing information. Make sure your comments are relevant do not waffle!!)

Fig. 9. Application form questions.

ments about interests (not what you think the reader will want to see on the form).

Remember to ensure that:

- your writing is legible
- facts are stated clearly
- everything is in a logical order.

ANSWERING QUESTIONS ABOUT HEALTH

Could you answer the following questions about your health?

What is your weight? _____   height? _____
Is your eyesight good/normal? _____
When did you last have a medical? _____
If you are a registered disabled person (RDP), do you know your registration number? _____
When does this need renewing? _____

Do you suffer or have you suffered from:

Diabetes	YES/NO
Heart trouble	YES/NO
Stomach trouble	YES/NO
Skin trouble	YES/NO
Any accident	YES/NO
Any rupture	YES/NO
Any muscle trouble	YES/NO
Any nerve trouble	YES/NO

Have you ever suffered from:
severe abdominal pains – hernia – dyspepsia – tuberculosis – rheumatic pains – epilepsy – fibrositis – sinusitis – dermatitis – congenital deformity – psychiatric problems?

(Did you get through this without the help of a dictionary? If so, well done!)

The usual question to check that your health is good is:

'Give details of any serious illness or time spent in hospital.'

Be accurate, brief and clear!!!

NAMING REFEREES

Consider carefully who your **referees** will be. If you can get someone known to the company to give you a reference, it should be to your advantage.

LISTING YOUR QUALIFICATIONS

Try to give a full picture when you state skills and qualifications. For instance, if you only put down 'Maths passed' when you have four other GCSEs at D grade, you must not expect the employer to be a mindreader!

USING EXTRA PAPER

If there is not enough space on the form, you will need to write on an **extra sheet** of paper. Most forms ask you to do this so that nothing important is missed out.

OVERHEARD IN THE PERSONNEL DEPARTMENT

'I just couldn't read his *writing*!'
'I know what you mean. He should have used block capitals.'
'One girl put her age down as 6702.'
'It must have been her phone number'
'Could be, but I think there are five digit numbers in that town. Also, she gave her address as the YWCA. I wonder if she's really got a permanent address?'
'That chap didn't put down a single thing under other interests and hobbies. I thought when reading his letter he sounded a pretty dull individual – hardly the sort of person we need in sales.'
'There was another one which was all filled in with a pale blue felt tip pen. Unfortunately, it wouldn't photocopy for our records department. Pity, really.'
'Still, there were some good ones . . .'
'Will you let me look through them, please?'

CHECKLIST

1. Read all the questions carefully before picking up your pen.

2. Don't write anything on the form until you fully understand the question and know exactly what you want to say.

3. Use black ink (better for photocopying).

4. If you are doubtful about any spelling, check beforehand (use a dictionary).

5. Ensure that your writing is legible and the facts accurate.

6. Don't forget to sign and date the form.

7. Read what you have written to ensure it is accurate, brief and clear. If possible, get someone else to check the completed form as well.

9
Using the Telephone

DEVELOPING A GOOD TELEPHONE TECHNIQUE

Some job advertisements ask applicants to telephone for further details (see Figure 10 on page 61). The quickest way to get rejected is to telephone without thinking about what you are going to say and what you intend asking. You may enjoy telephoning and even think you are good at it, but there are so many things that can go wrong if you are unprepared. It may be that an employer wants someone with a good telephone manner, in which case the person at the other end of the line will soon 'pick up' whether or not you have really thought about the phone call beforehand.

When using the telephone in applying for a job you should have a good technique so that time isn't wasted. Good telephone technique depends on whether you listen carefully, give essential information clearly and in logical order and are able to express yourself and develop a discussion about your strong points in relation to the work situation. You will be able to discuss more naturally if you find out a few details about the company *before* making the telephone call (what it does, how big it is, *etc.*).

PREPARING FOR YOUR PHONE CALL

Remember that the person at the other end of the line cannot see you, so you must make the most of your time. Your call has a 'once only' impact. If you make a hash of it, it is unlikely that you will get another opportunity to put things right.

- If you are using a public telephone, choose one which has few distractions (preferably away from a busy shopping area).

- Always make sure the telephone is in working order and that you have plenty of correct change.

- Before you make the call, write down essential facts about yourself on a small card which will fit in your pocket and be easy to hold in one hand.

- On the back of this card write prompters for questions about the job and/or company.

- Have a pen available in case you want to write something such as a telephone number which is best recorded rather than left to memory.

DEVELOPING YOUR VERBAL COMMUNICATION SKILLS

When you are using a telephone in connection with job hunting, you need to take stock of your communication skills.

- Do you find it easy to communicate?

- Do others ever have difficulty in understanding you?

- Do you speak clearly, at a reasonable speed with variation in the tone of your voice?

- Can you express yourself easily so that there can be an interesting discussion?

- Do you listen carefully so that you can 'pick up' key responses without any awkward pauses?

- Have you every listened to a recording of your voice? Do you sound interested and enthusiastic?

- Have you ever got anyone to be critical about your telephone manner?

If your answers to the above are all 'YES' then you must be good! If you do not know, perhaps now is the time to find out! If your answers are mainly 'NO' then you have to work on improving your verbal communication skills!

Example of bad technique

'Hallo, is that Stinton 6020?'

'No, this is Stinton 6220.'

'Oh, just a minute – (checks job advertisement). 'Sorry, yes, that's right, can I speak to Mr Robertson?'

'I'll just see if he's available. Who shall I say is calling?'

'It's about the job vacancy.'

'Yes, but who shall I say is calling?'

Oh, 'it's Chris – Chris Jones, calling about the job vacancy.'

'Thank you. I'm trying to connect you . . . I'm putting you through to Mr Robertson.'

'Is that Mr Robertson?'

'Speaking.'

'I'm calling about the job vacancy.'

'Which vacancy is that?'

'Oh, the one for the sales assistant.'

'I see. What is your name, please?'

'I'm sorry – can you hang on a minute? I've dropped my bag.'

BLANKLY TRAVEL LIMITED

require a

Clerical Assistant for the Accounts Department

Due to our continued expansion, we require a young person with an aptitude for figures to carry out general clerical duties in our busy accounts office. Previous experience not essential as training will be given. We offer a good salary, annual bonus, BUPA membership and holiday concessions.

Please telephone for an application form to:
MISS GLENDA JOHNSON
Tel: BLANKLY 12345 ext 123.

JUNIOR OFFICE CLERK
Required
9.00am–5.00pm, 5-day week

Interested in all clerical aspects including computer work. Own transport essential.

For interview please telephone Mr R. Roe 123-456-7890
THE SMITH GROUP SCHOOL LANE BLANKLY

YOUNG LADY wanted for full-time employment with dogs and occasional work with horses. Must be hard working and reliable to work with another girl. – Smithtown Horse Boarding Kennels. Tel: Blankley 12345.

YOUNG PERSON to work in busy Order Office. Good telephone manner essential. Will also include cutting and loading of glass. – Apply E. Jones between 9am and 4pm. Telephone 12345.

YOUNG PERSON required for leading roller shutter and sunblind company to train as a fitter. Please contact Mr Jones – Blankly 12345

SCHOOL LEAVER

Required
FOR THE POSITION OF FILING CLERK

Please contact Sue Smithson on LONG BLANKLY 12345 for an interview

---

Would you like to work away from home 4 days a week?

Earn a minimum of £80 per week. Are you 17 to 25 – fun loving

If so
Tel: Blankly 12345

TRAINEE SOUGHT. For interesting and varied work in friendly West Blankly office. We pay a bonus and have a good record of offering permanent positions on completion of training. WP ability essential. – Telephone 12345 for an appointment

---

Fig. 10. More examples of advertisements – asking you to telephone.

'I'm holding.'

'Yes – well – er . . .'

DEVELOPING YOUR LISTENING SKILLS

How good are your listening skills? Have you ever tried to assess them? There are so many reasons for *not* listening carefully, even when you make a telephone call! For instance, you may be trying to do two things at once, like fumbling for change or pen or paper. You could be distracted by other people trying to get your attention by waving at you or tapping on the call box. There could be extra loud noises of traffic, cars, planes, people shouting or singing.

When telephoning about a job you need to concentrate on what the person at the other end is saying, so that you can develop the conversation into a meaningful discussion.

CHECKLIST

1. Find out more about the company: what it does, *etc.* (get this information from the Jobcentre or local library).

2. **Know** and **plan** beforehand what you are going to say and ask.

3. Write down essential facts about yourself, in logical order, on a small card which you can hold in one hand.

4. On the back of this card write prompters for questions about the job and company *(eg* pay, hours).

5. Take stock of your communication skills; be aware of areas where you need to take extra care *(eg* shouting down the telephone).

6. If you use a public telephone, choose one where you are not likely to have distractions.

7. Make sure the telephone is in working order and have plenty of correct change handy.

8. Have a pen available to write down important names, numbers, *etc.*

9. Listen carefully.

10. Be **brief – clear – persuasive** – try to develop a meaningful discussion.

10
Calling at Business Premises

BENEFITS OF THE PERSONAL VISIT

It is worth considering whether calling at business premises might suit your style. If you feel more confident about discussing your application in person rather than writing, then this approach should appeal to you and it might be the best way to get that job.

This approach might also be appropriate to your circumstances, your job search area or where you live. For instance, if your job search area includes a concentrated number of employers, as on an industrial estate, it could save you the time and expense that would be involved in writing several letters. On the other hand, your job search area might be bigger and more widespread (say in a rural area) yet it is a small, close community where everyone knows everyone else. In such a situation, you would be expected to apply in person – not by writing.

Another advantage when calling at business premises is that by observing and listening carefully you should be able to get the 'feel' of the place. The way in which people go about their business and the physical aspects of the work situation will reflect the company's policies and procedures, including attitudes towards employees. This should help you decide what it might be like to work for that company.

An added advantage is that this occasion may develop into a **mini-interview**. Even if you don't see the employer, there is always a possibility that someone will pass on to him a few favourable comments about you.

Checklist
- **What firms** could you visit in your local area?

- Do you know their **addresses**?

- **Transport** – how would you get there?

- **Who** would you ask to see?

- Do you already **know** someone who works there?
- Could someone get you an **introduction**?
- What do you know about these firms' **products** and **services**?
- Do you have any of their **brochures**?
- What kind of **job** could you see yourself doing there?
- Are they **open** in the daytime, evenings, at weekends?:

MAKING THE MOST OF THIS EXPERIENCE

To make the most of this opportunity, you need to achieve a good impact; therefore you should consider what kind of an impression you are likely to make. The important issues will include:

- your appearance
- the way you express yourself
- the extent to which you have prepared for this event and organised information about yourself.

You should aim at creating a good impression so that, when the short-listing for interview is done, there will be a likeable 'face' to go with your application.

First impressions count

When you are searching for a job, first impressions are most important. You will need to be self-critical about your appearance, making sure you look neat, clean and acceptable. This can be a problem if you decide to call in at several companies during one day, particularly if it involves you in considerable walking or cycling and it is a windy or wet day.

Being prepared

Although it is important to give the right physical impression, you will only make a good impact if you have thought carefully about what is likely to happen, so that you can react naturally and at the same time handle the situation to your advantage. Take with you (for each company you visit) either a typed CV or a written record of your name, address, telephone number, age and brief details of your work experience, skills, education and interests. At the bottom of this information, print the names, address and telephone number of two people who will give you a reference (try to include the name of someone who knows you in a work situation). Although it will cost you, it might even be worthwhile to include your photograph.

Communication skills and a positive attitude

Know beforehand what you are going to say when you get inside the business premises, where your first contact is likely to be the receptionist. Be polite and speak clearly. Pay careful attention to non-verbal communication, listen carefully and look interested. Aim at having a realistic attitude and quietly confident manner; be sincere in your intention and hopeful about being given a formal opportunity to present your application.

BEING AWARE OF THE RISKS

Calling at business premises can be risky and, if things go wrong, you may just as well write off any chances of future employment with that company. You should try to prepare yourself for the unexpected because you never know how the employer or his/her staff will react to you. For instance, you may call at what you think is a reasonable time of the day but you find it is inconvenient and nobody wants to talk to you. Whatever you do in those circumstances, you will be taking a risk, more so if you try to force an interview.

Recognising the difficult situations

It should help you if you can recognise the danger signals so that you can prevent the situation from worsening and be able to handle things with some sensitivity. For example, if the receptionist has to answer the telephone, what would you do? Thumbs down if you continue to look at her and obviously listen to her conversation? *Thumbs up* if you politely back away, turn round or look elsewhere!

Improving your chances

If you want to improve those skills which help you to be sensitive to situations and people you should consider certain points:

- Have you an expressive face? (Sometimes that can land you in trouble and adversely affect your job prospects.)

- How good are your observation skills? (Do you always read notices such as 'NO SMOKING'?)

- How perceptive are you about situations and/or people?

- Can you recognise key points in conversation and develop these to your advantage?

- Are you likely to be too 'pushy', or over-confident, or too chatty?

You should think about the different types of situations you might meet when you call at business premises. Aim to be flexible in your approach so that you minimise the risk of things not turning out right for you.

CONSIDERING THE EMPLOYER'S VIEWPOINT

If you decide to call at business premises, you should bear in mind that there are some employers who *insist* on having written letters of application for jobs, whilst others *prefer* written applications and discourage casual callers. However, the majority of employers tend to accept that these days, when jobs are scarce, there will be some people who use their initiative and put a great deal of effort into their job search, including calling at business premises. These are the ones you want to establish contact with. Your local Jobcentre may be able to advise you of some employers' attitudes to casual callers and they should at least be aware of those who insist on written applications. However, for the most part, you have to play this by ear and be prepared for different reactions.

Planning pays off

If your approach is planned you are more likely to get a co-operative reaction from the employer or his/her her representative. Generally, if an employer thinks that you have taken the trouble to find out about the company, then gone out of your way to visit the place, he/she is likely to consider your application – if only briefly! There could be an advantage to the employer in seeing you without being committed to a full interview. This factor would certainly appeal to someone who regards him/herself as a good judge of people by appearance and manner, to whom seeing a person is much better than reading a letter of application. Also, there might be a vacancy coming up in the near future and, if an employer thought you suitable, he/she would save a considerable amount of time and money in not having to advertise or pay out interview expenses.

CHECKLIST

1. Select this approach if you prefer to discuss your application in person rather than by writing.

2. Check with your Jobcentre – ask for brief information about employers.

3. Be self-critical about your appearance and verbal and non-verbal communication skills.

4. Take with you, for each company you visit, your CV or written personal details.

5. Know beforehand what you are going to say – plan to achieve a good impact.

11
Handling The Employment Interview

ASSESSING YOURSELF

One of the most difficult tasks is to assess yourself objectively. However, as you acquire experience it is usually easier to identify what you are good at and what needs improving upon, possibly by training.

You should start by making a list of **strong points** and **weak points** (see Figure 11). When doing this you need to be realistic and honest with yourself, otherwise it becomes a meaningless exercise. You will then be able to identify certain qualities not usually revealed in school reports and certificates obtained.

For instance, you may not be academically minded and your exam grades are low; however, you have certain qualities that are more important to some employers than the ability to do well in exams. A sales assistant needs a pleasant personality to encourage customers to return and buy more goods. A job involving repetitive work requires someone with the right kind of temperament – not someone who gets bored by doing the same thing.

Although most adverts require you to write, nowadays an increasing number of employers want you to telephone.

- Study the advert carefully.
- Think about your strong points in relation to the job.
- Then prepare for presentation by letter or telephone.

USING THE JOB SPECIFICATION

Most large organisations have formal, written job specifications (or job descriptions) and it is common to see an advert which invites you to write for an application form and further details. (See Figures 12 and 13 for examples.)

As well as being informative, a job specification enables you to have a very positive approach to the interview because you can study it beforehand and make a note of any queries. Then, at the interview,

SELF-ASSESSMENT LIST as at April 9X

Strong points

Cheerful
Tidy , clean
Sensible -so I'm told
Always on time -punctual
Can be left on my own
    and get on with work
Get on with people
Like working with my hands
Don't mind doing odd jobs

Weak areas

Sometimes impatient
Bad loser
Moody at times
Poor at spelling
  - have to ask
Whistle too much
    at times

Fig. 11. Example of self-assessment.

1. Write up Sales Day Book and post entries to Sales Ledger.
2. Write up Purchase Day Book and post entries to Purchase Ledger.
3. Prepare PAYE returns.
4. Prepare VAT returns.
5. Draw cheques for wages and salaries.
6. Write up Cash Book and reconcile with weekly bank statements.
7. Write up Petty Cash Book and keep Petty Cash Box.
8. Pay in cash and cheques each day to the Bank.
9. Prepare invoices and monthly statements to customers.
10. Assist the Accounts Manager as required.

Fig. 12. Typical job specification for a book-keeper.

HOW WOULD YOU ASSESS YOURSELF?

STRONG POINTS	WEAK AREAS
_____	_____
_____	_____
_____	_____
_____	_____
_____	_____
_____	_____
_____	_____
_____	_____
_____	_____
_____	_____
_____	_____

you are more likely to have a meaningful discussion of the job in relation to your suitability. Unfortunately many people just read the job specification and don't bother to use it as a valuable **key to discussion** of their strengths.

(a)   Do all filing for the secretarial pool.
(b)   Check stationery supplies each week.
(c)   Fill in departmental job cards each day.
(d)   Assist with general copy-typing.
(e)   Assist the Office Manageress.
(f)   Make tea, run errands and take messages.

Fig. 13. Typical job specification for an office junior.

If the information about the job is 'in the head' of the interviewer, listen carefully. Get a mental picture of the job and identify the key points.

THINKING ABOUT POSSIBLE INTERVIEW QUESTIONS

You should be prepared to discuss any aspect concerning your suitability for the job and adjustment to that particular work situation. Expect to talk about school achievements, work experience, interests and hobbies, relationships with other people and aspects of your home situation which might affect your work.

You may be asked about your hopes and ambitions for the future (difficult to answer unless you have thought about it previously). The interviewer may ask 'What job would you like to be doing in, say, eight years time?' If you are really ambitious, you may think 'Your job!' but don't like to say so for fear of sounding cheeky. You need to think about such questions and decide how you are going to answer them.

PREPARING FOR YOUR INTERVIEW

Before the interview you should prepare a **list** of what you want to know about the job and working relationships with the other employees (see Figure 14). Job details are usually clearly described but most interviewers rarely comment on **working relationships** unless there are special conditions ('you will have to work closely with . . .'). It is worthwhile considering this aspect and making a note of a few basic questions such as 'How many people will I be working with?', 'What age group are they?'

You also need to think about your **appearance** and **performance** at the interview. Your performance will depend on how effectively

- How many other people would I be working with? What age group are they?
- Who will show me what to do?
- Would you expect me to wear overalls?
- Will I get chance to learn several jobs?
- What kind of training will I get? How long will it last? What happens at the end of training?
- Will you expect me to continue with education?
- What do I need to do to improve my chances of getting this job?

NOTE: If there is a formal job description or written details of the job and company, try to relate most of your questions to the information given.

Fig. 14. Questions you might ask at an interview.

you communicate with the interviewer, whether or not you are sincere and express yourself clearly and freely. Your appearance should be neat, clean and acceptable.

Interviews – How ready are YOU?

❏ What shall I wear?	❏ Relevant hobbies?
❏ Clean and tidy?	❏ Qualifications?
❏ Feeling fit and well?	❏ Copy of your CV?
❏ A copy of the job ad?	❏ References available?
❏ Knowledge of the work?	❏ When could you start?
❏ Thought about the job?	❏ Pay expectations?
❏ Some questions to ask?	❏ Check time and place?
❏ Clear ambitions?	❏ Know how to get there?
❏ Work experience?	❏ Enough time to get there?

Any interview is partly a science, partly an art! The science part is the extent to which it can be planned and the preparation involved. The art part is the way you handle the interview – cope with the situation.

QUESTIONS YOU MIGHT BE ASKED BY THE INTERVIEWER

If a school-leaver

What/How do you feel about leaving school? What did you like most about school? What did you achieve? What do you think about your school reference?

General questions

Tell me about yourself (most difficult to answer if you haven't thought about it beforehand). Why do you want this job? (Be honest; not afraid of saying 'I *want work*!') What do you know about us? (Get to know as much as you can about the company beforehand; be prepared to say how you found the information). Have you ever done any part-time work (holidays, weekends, paper rounds, *etc.*)? If so, tell me about it.

How do you get on with other people? Any problems? Have you ever had to deal with any difficult people? What happened?

Tell me about the things you do in a typical day. (This could be an important question if you have been out of work for a lengthy period; the employer will want to know if you have done something useful with your time.)

What do your parents think about your applying for this job? Do you have to help out at home? If so, what do you have to do? Have you any younger brothers or sisters? If so, do you have to help them?

Are you a practical person? Do you like working with your hands? Any hobbies or interests? How do you feel about ... overtime? attending college? working on your own? working in a small office? having to stay on at short notice to finish a job? having several junior jobs to do – be at people's beck and call? making tea every morning and afternoon? having to run errands for me? working with several older people?

What do you think about ... (a current topic which is important either to the company or you or the local community)?

Being yourself

Try to remember that an employment interview is a two-way exchange of information, so it is important for you to let the interviewer know as much as possible about you. In spite of the pressures often associated with an employment interview, try to be natural. There is no point in pretending to be someone else because this will only create a doubt in the mind of the interviewer. If you are yourself, it will help the interview develop into a free-flowing discussion.

THE INTERVIEWER'S ASSESSMENT OF YOU

An interviewer has to decide whether you can do the job, with training if necessary, and fit in with the other employees. A good interviewer, wanting to be selective, will have an **objective assessment plan** and you will be graded depending on how you match up to the job requirements (see Figure 15).

If the '**Five-Fold Plan**' is used, the assessment areas are: Qualifications and Experience; Brains and Innate Abilities; Impact; Motivation; Adjustment. In a large organisation you will probably

Fig. 15. Example of interviewer assessment form.

have to complete selection tests (see below) and your potential ability will be assessed for the future.

As well as the employers who use this scientific approach to selection, there are others who rely mainly on their hunches and you may get a job simply because you give the impression of being the right sort of person to do that job (hurrah for the 'vibes' working for you!).

'He had a *very* nice personality. I think he would fit in very well.'

'I thought he had a bit of a chip on his shoulder. We'll put a question mark on that one.'

'She asked some very good questions, didn't she? I think she'd be very good in dealing with our suppliers.'

TAKING SELECTION TESTS

Many employers wanting more information about applicants will give them selection tests, which may vary from simple mental arithmetic (*eg* 'What is the VAT on . . . ?') to comprehensive **aptitude tests** which are used to identify your potential and ability to cope with skills training.

Types of tests

If the job you are interested in involves either specialist or lengthy formal training, you can expect to have to complete a series of tests, both practical and written. These will probably include dexterity tests such as Pin/Peg Board, to test the way and time it is likely to take you to handle work. Then there is the pattern recognition test, where you are required to slot different shaped pieces of wood into their respective positions (see Figure 16). Written tests such as the G10 and V10 identify not only your literacy and numeracy but also your intelligence and mechanical aptitude.

Completing the 'picture' of you

If you have to do such tests, remember it doesn't necessarily depend on how clever you are or how good at writing. Most employers use carefully prepared, often nationally known, practical tests to complete their 'picture' of you, including those aspects which are not covered by your education results, the application or the interview.

Fig. 16. Pattern recognition.

Attending the test session

If you apply for a job with a large organisation, most probably you will be invited to attend a half-day selection test session, when you and numerous other applicants will have to complete several written and practical tests.

Tests as part of vocational guidance

When you have an in-depth interview with your careers adviser, they may ask you to complete several tests that reveal your verbal and numerical reasoning, visual reasoning and mechanical aptitude. In fact, if you receive any vocational guidance counselling, you will have to do several tests so that you can be advised about suitable training to realise your full potential.

Medical examinations

If you apply for employment with a company in the food industry, you are required by law to have a thorough medical examination, including X-rays and blood tests. Many other organisations also require you to have some sort of physical test (*eg* for colour-blindness) before confirming your employment.

CHECKLIST

1. Plan and prepare a list of questions before the interview: what will you want to know about the job and other people in the work situation?

2. Consider the kind of questions you might be asked and *be prepared to discuss* any aspect of your suitability for the job and adjustment to the work situation.

3. Plan to be punctual for the interview; be self-critical about your appearance (ask others' advice and comments). Look neat, clean and acceptable.

4. Expect to be assessed on interview behaviour.
   (a) Be courteous and polite.
   (b) Listen carefully.
   (c) Speak clearly.
   (d) Establish eye contact (look at the interviewer without 'fixing him'). Look interested and smile!
   (e) Pay careful attention to non-verbal communication by being aware of mannerisms that might irritate some people.
   (f) Try to establish a mutual exchange of comments and discuss freely. Be natural!

12
Maintaining your
Job Search Programme

KEEPING A LIST OF EMPLOYERS AND POTENTIAL EMPLOYERS

If you keep an **updated list** of employers and potential employers, you will be able to keep your finger on the pulse of possible employment. In any event, these days it is wise to have another option and be able to take alternative action – just in case!

If you are unemployed, this list can save you a lot of time and effort. It also means you do not have to rely on Lady Luck – you can use the list in a positive way and plan your job search programme in an organised manner. You don't need to go back to square one just because you aren't successful in getting a job the first time you approach an employer.

UPDATING YOUR FILES

It is, of course, most important to keep the details of your list up-to-date so that you can follow up at any time and be aware of possible vacancies arising. So the first thing you need to do to start the list is get, from either the Jobcentre or the main library, the name, address/location, type (manufacture or service) and approximate size of all local companies.

Once you have this basic information, you can add to the list other facts that will further influence your job opportunities. For instance, Jobcentre staff or librarians are likely to comment on some, if not most, of the companies, particularly the Jobcentre who probably have several personal contacts; it is a bonus if you can find out who is responsible for recruitment.

You can add special notes (useful information obtained from hearsay, local papers, advertisements, *etc.*) and refer to the travel distance and cost involved. In this way you can build up a very helpful **reference file** which will be the basis for your personal job search programme.

- Be organised and systematic.

- Keep records so that you can find things quickly.

- Try every source of information you can find.

- Keep adding information to your collection.

KEEPING A RECORD OF THOSE EMPLOYERS WHO HAVE YOUR NAME ON THEIR WAITING LIST

If you are ever asked whether you wish to have your name kept on a waiting list, say 'Yes, please!' and be prepared to follow up this sign of approval that you are worthwhile being considered for employment with that company.

Please do not assume that you should then sit back and wait for them to contact you. It is up to you to use this experience in a positive and, hopefully, eventually successful way by:

- making a brief record of the company's rating as an employer

- following up in a planned approach.

In this way you sustain the company's interest in you by letting them know about your keenness to work for them.

Noting the details

Aim at a simple yet clear record. Note any special details including employee benefits such as free protective clothing/equipment; cheap 'seconds'; training; opportunities for advancement. Avoid recording only details which might change, when there are other essential facts. For instance, 'X' company pays £20 per week more than other employers; travel may well involve cost of £18 per week. (See Figure 17.)

```
Name of firm: _____
Address:  _____
          _____
Phone no:_____
Personal contact:_____
Job applied for:  _____
Approx. rates of pay:_____
Training opportunities:  _____
Notes:  _____
```

Fig. 17. Recording employer details.

It is best to keep your record brief, either on the back of the company's letter (invitation to interview, *etc.*) or on a card. Whichever method of reference you choose, it is advisable to keep the information in a file marked **Employers Waiting List** or something similar.

Following up

The important thing is to have a brief, clear reference which can be updated and used in your job search. Thus, if you haven't heard from such an employer for several months, you can approach the company and remind them, in the nicest way, that you are still keen to join the organisation. Usually such positive action yields success!

ESTABLISHING YOUR PERSONAL JOB SEARCH PROGRAMME

Once you have compiled a list of employers, it will be possible to decide a plan of action and initiate your personal job search programme. This needs to be organised in advance, as a **weekly diary** (see Figure 18), indicating basic information such as time of interview, place, company, together with other relevant details (4-star company; good prospects; job sounds great, *etc.*).

Initially it can be fairly simple, comparable to a working diary where the aim is accuracy concerning time, date, venue, name of person or company involved. However, in areas of high unemployment this plan needs to include other influencing factors. For instance, if local newspaper headlines are 'X Company redundancies!' the employment chances are unlikely to be good. If, however, the headlines are 'X Company – additional investment of £3m!' then there should be good employment prospects.

Reviewing progress

To use your experience and make your efforts worthwhile, you should look critically at your personal job search programme at the end of each week and every month to see how you are progressing.

At its best, this action plan can be developed into an organised and meaningful job search programme. Furthermore, it is good thinking to use such a plan because it encourages you to organise your time in a constructive way. Also, your concentrated efforts are likely to result in the most successful approach toward job hunting.

Developing your plan of action

If you want to intensify your job search, it will inevitably involve

Day/Date/Time	Action	to/person involved	Company concerned	Venue	Job vacancy/result	Follow-up/comments
MON 2 Jun	Letter	C. Moore Personnel Officer	Excell Ltd Park Road Durham D10 2L		Accept offer to be put on their waiting list	Note for future 5 star company
TUE 3 Jul 9.30 a.m	Interview Selection Tests	Report to Training Officer	Easi-Fit Ltd Industrial Estate	Training Centre	Trainee Computer Operator	Doubtful – 10 on shortlist
THU 5 Jul 2.30 pm	Interview	T. Norton	Norton, Bite & Boff Solicitors Winsley Road	⟶ Office	Junior Clerical Assistant	C.A. managed – should be offered this – might I accept – not sure would suit job. Action ⟶ after interview, phone C.A.
FRI 6 Jun	Phone (30261)	Career Adviser				

TUE   Jobcentre a.m.   Library p.m.
WED   See / phone Career   Jobcentre p.m.
THU   Library – local paper ads/mags ?
FRI   Action any poss job   – telephone, write, call in

Fig. 18. Personal job search programme.

consideration of several 'possible' jobs at the same time. This might worry you. You might even find yourself in a position where you feel uneasy and doubtful about discussing other pending interviews; consequently your comments are likely to be vague, even evasive.

You need to be aware of such pitfalls when developing your plan of action. From your point of view, you are being realistic *and* modest by not assuming you will get that particular job. Also, if you wait and apply for one vacancy at a time, you may well be missing out on a more suitable job whilst your application is being processed. This could be very time-consuming if there are a few hundred applications to be sorted.

Adopting the sensible approach

Prospective employers will realise that it is not easy to get a job these days, so that if you are keen to work you *must* follow up several vacancies at once. Most employers do not lose interest when they find out that other interviews are 'in the pipeline', provided you are honest and sincere in your intentions.

However, beware of being tempted to use other interviews as a bargaining ploy to force an offer of employment. The other sensitive situation is if you are awaiting results of another interview. In either instance, there is a need for planning beforehand what your approach is going to be, bearing in mind that the effective employment interview should reflect a situation where there is frank and open discussion between you and your prospective boss.

CHECKLIST

1. Prepare a list of employers and potential employers.
   (a) Get basic details of these from your Jobcentre or main library.
   (b) Add other facts which will influence job opportunities with these firms.
   (c) Keep details up to date.

2. Prepare a record of those employers who have your name on their waiting list
   (a) Keep a file labelled 'Employers Waiting List'.
   (b) Keep brief, clear references which can be updated and used in your job search.
   (c) Use the information to follow up and remind those employers that you are still interested in employment with them.

3. Establish your personal job search programme (plan of action).
   (a) Organise in advance a weekly working diary showing time, date, venue, name of person and company involved and other special notes/influencing factors.
   (b) Prepare an organised and meaningful job search programme.

4. Develop your plan of action.
   (a) Plan your job search – several jobs at one time.
   (b) Show you are keen to work – be open about following up several jobs at once.
   (c) Be honest and sincere about your intentions.
   (d) Plan your approach beforehand.
   (e) Aim at an effective employment interview – frank and open discussion.

13
Getting Practice and Help

Although practice doesn't always make you perfect, it *does* get you used to situations. It also helps you develop your job search skills.

LETTER WRITING

This is an occasion when you have to determine clearly what you aim to get out of the exercise. Also, those who help must try to ignore the fact that you are the writer. They should react naturally and instinctively, as if they had received the letter from someone unknown.

All concerned should agree that the essentials of a good letter of application will include:

- legible handwriting
- correct spelling
- appropriate punctuation
- style reflecting you as an individual
- courtesy, including prompt reply to company letter
- good business format
- balanced paragraphs.

You need to **practise** and your family and friends need to **react** instinctively – they should not take time in reaching conclusions.
Practise *describing your strong points without seeming big-headed.*
Example: My references will confirm that I am a good timekeeper and conscientious at work.
Practise *getting over the right message.*
Example: Given the opportunity, I intend working hard because I *want* to do this kind of job.

In short, you need to **practise** *communicating your personal characteristics and abilities honestly and sincerely, emphasising your strong points without sounding too full of your own importance.*
Aim to get the appropriate impact on paper!

EMPLOYMENT INTERVIEW SITUATIONS

This is a sensitive area and calls for considerable thought about the people who are involved and what is going to be achieved. It is best to get friends rather than family to help because it is usually difficult for relatives to be impartial. On the other hand, members of the family, particularly parents, are likely to be more experienced and aware of the pitfalls.

How many helpers?

It is usually most helpful if there are only two people because even a small group can get too chatty, so that it becomes difficult to exercise self-control and keep quiet. Additionally, if there are only two people involved, the 'one-to-one' discussion is more likely to be realistic. If you are a nervous, shy or quiet person, you should get much more out of this experience and it is bound to help you when it comes to the real interview.

Of course there *are* advantages in having a few observers and listeners because these people could make some useful comments. It really depends on the people concerned and how committed they are to helping you and being constructive in what they say. Usually, unless a group situation is controlled by someone experienced in such **role play** situations, it is more likely that negative comments will be made about the interviewee's (your) performance. Also you are less likely to be natural because you will be aware of those watchers and feel self-conscious about everything you do and say.

Preparing and planning

Whatever is decided about the number of people taking part, it is essential that:

- You establish beforehand what the interview situation is so that the purpose may be clearly identified.

- Your interviewer prepares some sort of plan: decides on a few questions and what areas are to be discussed (they should aim to cover only a few points).

- You (as interviewee) have a plan; aim at referring to your strong points and be prepared for discussion of relevant areas.

Learning from the experience

If possible, **tape the interview**. No one can argue with a recording of what is said. It will also ensure that you can have a rational discussion about the areas to be improved upon.

The overall aim should be that your practice employment interview is meaningful and worthwhile. At worst, this sensitive situation could end a good friendship because you do not see eye-to-eye about certain points. At best, you could both learn from the experience and develop the skills necessary for an effective interview.

USING THE TELEPHONE

Although a beneficial exercise for would-be telephone job searchers, this can become a fun area that rapidly gets out of hand and is regarded as a big joke. If you *do* decide to practise using the telephone, you and anyone involved must be prepared to concentrate and imagine it is a 'for real' phone-in.

Bearing this in mind, you need a typical situation so that the person who 'answers' your telephone call knows whom they represent and can discuss the job details. Therefore each of you must have a copy of the information concerning the company and the job, so that it will be realistic.

Organising yourself

Before you start, you need to organise your efforts and consider the following:

- The **physical arrangement** is important as the usual family situation makes it necessary for both of you to be in the same room. It may even involve special arrangements to get a room to yourselves. However, you must *not* be able to see each other whilst you are talking, so – back to back, and *no cheating*!

- Ensure that the **tape recorder** is working efficiently. If you find at the end of the conversation that it wasn't working, hard luck! Make sure it is switched on to record the conversation.

- **Record** the complete conversation.

- Before you play back, have a **brief discussion** and try to be constructively critical about each other's performance, even though more importance is attached to the job seeker's performance.

- Have pen and paper handy to make **notes** during the playback.

- **Play back:** listen to the complete record of the conversation (*DO NOT STOP TAPE*).

- After playback, **compare notes and discuss** the complete situation, referring to specific parts of the conversation.

Getting experienced people involved

Perhaps this is an occasion when you might coax some of the family to help you. It would certainly be useful if more experienced people could be persuaded to take part, if only in a general discussion. However, no matter who is involved, this is an area where you always learn something about your telephone technique and manner of communicating. It is well worth doing!

CHECKLIST

1. Letter writing:
   (a) Practise the essentials of writing a good business letter: legible writing; correct spelling; appropriate punctuation; good business format; balanced paragraphs.
   (b) Practise writing about yourself; describing your strong points, getting over the right message in a brief, sincere way.

2. Employment interview situations:
   (a) Have only two people involved: you, being interviewed, and another as interviewer.
   (b) One-to-one discussion; each has an interview plan, according to role.
   (c) Tackle only a few discussion areas.
   (d) Preferably tape the discussion.
   (e) Aim to have a practice interview which is meaningful and worthwhile, so that you will both learn from the experience and develop the skills necessary for an employment interview situation.

3. Using the telephone:
   (a) Clearly establish the role play situation, each having written details of the company and the job.
   (b) Organise your efforts: prepare room, back-to-back, tape recorder in good working order.
   (c) Concentrate: imagine it is a 'for-real' phone-in situation.
   (d) Record the complete conversation.
   (e) Briefly discuss before playback.
   (f) Play back *all* the taped discussion. **Listen** and make notes, if necessary.
   (g) Afterwards, compare notes and discuss the complete situation; refer to tape.

14
Making Good Use of your Time

DEVELOPING YOUR SKILLS

Frequently it is that additional skill which is the deciding factor in getting the job, so it is to your advantage if you use your time constructively.

Some of the possibilities are obvious. For instance, if you are interested in getting a full-time clerical job, you need to find out the best, quickest and least costly way of acquiring skills associated with working in an office. You can attend a college to get **word processing and computer skills** (if you are under 18 years old it won't cost anything at a College of Further Education). Several organisations offer short, intensive courses so you can acquire skills within a minimum time, at a price. The best approach is to find out what facilities are available, through your Jobcentre or local library.

Your driving licence
The ability to drive is a practical skill which is most useful when searching for a job, as well as being highly desirable for personal reasons. You may not have passed your driving test but if you are able to write down that you have a provisional driving licence it reflects your ambitions/intentions and gives you an advantage over someone who hasn't bothered.

First aid
One skill which tends to be thought of as an interest rather than being related to work concerns First Aid. If you are a qualified First Aider, trained in St John Ambulance work, it would undoubtedly have a great influence on your getting a job. Do not forget that all firms need to be covered for Health and Safety regulations.

Correspondence courses
Another consideration is whether to take a correspondence course. Nowadays there are reputable organisations such as the International

Correspondence School and the Business Correspondence School which offer several correspondence courses leading to recognised examinations. Obviously a correspondence course favours the kind of skills which involve writing, including accountancy, ranging from GCSEs and languages to professional qualifications (in which case studies are related to the respective professional institute).

Skills training
Some national organisations offer skills training. Typical examples would include the Territorial Army, RAF Cadets, Naval Cadets, Sea Scouts and Rangers as well as organised youth club activities (working for the Duke of Edinburgh Awards.)

GAINING EXPERIENCE THROUGH VOLUNTARY WORK

Voluntary work is **not** doing something for nothing – there are skills which you can develop indirectly as a result of experience. A good example of this is doing work with local voluntary organisations. It is surprising how much information and expertise you can acquire in, say, organising and administration, social skills, getting on with different types of people or manual skills such as helping to decorate for old people. You may not be trained to do the job but you pick up the skills by watching other people do it, then you have a go yourself!

KEEPING FIT FOR WORK

Many unemployed people don't realise they need to keep fit for work. It is so very easy to get unfit! If you are unemployed and keep getting rejected for jobs, it seems natural to stay in bed in the morning, thinking 'What have I got to get up for?' Well, when you do that, probably someone shouts at you to get up, and it's not just because that someone thinks it will be good for you not to develop idle habits (although of course that is true!). It's because someone knows that young people need to be into physical things – action!!

How fit do you need to be?
It is not suggested that you become a sports fanatic or athlete, although these would involve getting very fit and at the same time provide most absorbing interests. However, you *do* need to be realistic and ask yourself how fit are you? Most of all, can you complete a hard day's work (even in a job not reckoned to be physical) and

keep up a good performance for the rest of the week.

In some jobs, the demand for a certain standard of fitness can be exhausting. Those jobs are obviously physical – labouring, manual work, *etc.* However, every job demands a certain fitness, even though at first this may not be apparent. For instance, a sales assistant is able to move about the shop but has to stand all day. A factory machinist has to sit on the same seat, in the same place, with the same body movements, to do his/her job each day at work.

Impressing potential employers

When a potential employer assesses you, he/she is likely to rate this fitness factor fairly high. If you turn up for the interview looking pale, with 'bags' under your eyes, giving a general impression of being tired out, it is not surprising if there is a big question mark at the side of 'fitness rating'. In such circumstances, the typical question would be 'What do you do with yourself all day?'

Don't let your body get used to staying in bed until 10 or 11 a.m., then phasing out the day to make it last. Make good use of your time; have a healthy attitude towards keeping fit for work!

Using local sports and leisure facilities

If you live within a city area or a place where there is high unemployment, it is advisable to find out from your local library or Recreation Centre whether or not there is a scheme operating whereby, as an unemployed young person, you may enjoy leisure facilities such as swimming, snooker, badminton, table-tennis – *free of charge!*

Some cities have excellent schemes to help in this way. Sheffield is one example. It encourages the unemployed to keep fit in mind and body – hopefully for work! Sheffield offers a '**Passport to Leisure**'!

This concession is only available for people who live within the city boundary. The Recreation Department produces a series of leaflets which cover different leisure activities (*eg* swimming and sports centre facilities) with useful explanatory notes on how to apply. When you are accepted you get your 'Passport to Leisure' (a pass which includes your photograph) and become eligible to use all the facilities either free of charge or for a small cost.

KNOWING YOUR SUPPORT SERVICES

All too frequently, young people find out about government benefits and local supportive facilities as a last resort, by which time they may have unnecessarily experienced strained circumstances.

The extent to which young people *know* about available financial aid tends to vary considerably, depending on whether they live in a rural or city area and on other people who are involved in preparation for leaving school and starting work. Occasionally newspapers inform about important issues such as 'Claiming Benefits' but generally this kind of information is communicated by teachers, careers advisers, youth clubs and, of course, parents. You may be lucky in getting to know about the various ways in which help is available, including explanatory leaflets. However, it may well be a case of 'If you don't ask, you won't get . . .', so you need to have some idea of where to go for information.

Using the DSS

If you want information about **financial benefits**, you should visit your local DSS where the staff should be able to advise and help, particularly if you have a special problem. They will put you in touch with the appropriate community service (*eg* Social Services). They also issue free pamphlets which explain clearly what is involved in such important matters as claiming state benefits whilst unemployed, supplementary benefit, *etc*. These pamphlets are published and updated by the **Central Office of Information (COI)** – very necessary nowadays because of changing government regulations.

Citizens' Advice Bureaux

Another source of help is the Citizens' Advice Bureaux, where you may get free and impartial advice about a wide variety of issues including personal welfare, legal aid and financial problems. The CAB also supply informative leaflets as well as advising you how to go about things. They can put you in touch with other organisations (such as the DSS) including private local organisations and charities which are prepared to assist young people.

The important thing here is to know what assistance is available and how to go about getting help when it is needed.

> Decide what to do,
> to learn something new;
> Keep busy, keep fit
> – then you won't feel blue.
> Make leisure a pleasure
> till that job is in view!

15
Working Abroad

THINKING ABOUT PERSONAL CONSIDERATIONS

Working abroad not only involves considering legal requirements, there are also personal issues which are particularly important if your contract covers two years or more.

Although your contract will refer to pay, you will need to bear in mind those other factors which have a considerable influence on your money. For example, if the **cost of living** is extraordinarily high (as it is in some European countries) you will find it difficult to save and, even if you do save, there may be problems in transferring your savings back home. Other influences on your money will be the rate of exchange and tax regulations.

Spending and saving

You will want to estimate how much you are likely to spend on **accommodation and food**, even when your contract states that these are provided free. Your estimate will presumably reflect your intended lifestyle. For instance, if you are highly motivated to save, then you will be prepared to exist on whatever is provided free of charge; on the other hand, you may like your extra comforts, in which case you will need to be prepared to pay for these. Similarly with **leisure** pursuits, which may also involve legal restrictions (*eg* alcohol is banned in many Middle Eastern countries).

Insurance

Another issue in your contract will concern insurance. Although your employer will advise on this, it is as well to check every aspect in relation to your particular needs because people have different ideas about the extent to which they should be insured. Obviously a lot depends on the country and work situation (some countries, such as Australia, require you to have health insurance). If in doubt, it is advisable to contact one of the specialist insurance companies.

You also need to bear in mind that your position could quickly be affected by changes in the **political** scene.

EMPLOYMENT OPPORTUNITIES IN EU COUNTRIES

The big advantage about working in one of the EU Countries is that there is legally free movement of labour, therefore you don't need a work permit. However, you **do** have to **register** with the local authorities concerned in order to get a **residence permit**. Usually this involves supplying some written evidence to confirm that you have been offered at least three months' employment.

Getting information from the Jobcentre

It is a good idea to contact your Jobcentre because occasionally they have details of vacancies in EU countries. You can also obtain from them a useful leaflet, *Working Abroad*, which tells you how to get a job abroad and what kind of things you need to consider before accepting employment. Additionally, they should be able to supply you with names and addresses of agencies and British firms that have branches in EU countries.

Applying for jobs abroad

If you decide to write to these contacts, it is advisable to include an International Reply Coupon (obtainable from Post Offices), your CV and comprehensive details of what you can offer, as well as the type of work you are seeking. Should you use the services of an employment agency abroad, remember that you and your prospective employer will be charged a fee for this service.

SHORT-TERM WORK OPPORTUNITIES

There are likely to be more opportunities for short-term employment, particularly seasonal or summer vacation work in industries such as catering, hotels, etc. Some organisations arrange employment on an exchange basis; for instance, the Hotel Careers Centre, Bournemouth runs international schemes, on a quota basis, for young people in the catering industry. It is possible to find work, usually as a junior commis waiter/waitress, for periods of up to one year in most European countries.

Other ways of looking for work abroad

You could also reply to adverts in British or foreign newspapers or trade journals. However, as it is easy to travel in EU countries, you may decide to do so and try to get work 'on spec'. If you do this, you should be prepared for problems such as poor pay, uninteresting and hard manual work, difficulties in finding accommodation, considerable travel and expense in getting to work.

Whichever way you choose to carry out your job search, remember that if unemployment increases in your chosen country, it will be much more difficult to get any type of work!

EMPLOYMENT OPPORTUNITIES IN COUNTRIES OTHER THAN THE EU

If you are interested in working abroad for a lengthy period, you should first of all contact the foreign Embassy concerned, who will advise you on the existing situation and relevant **regulations**.

Regulations concerning work and residence permits differ from country to country but basically they depend on:

* having a positive job offer
* being able to speak the language
* having pre-arranged accommodation.

Usually your prospective employer will have to apply for your **work permit**. In Third World countries each company is granted permits on a **quota** basis and, as the rules are strictly enforced, you are only likely to be accepted for a specified time of 2–3 years. In Australia, it would be 3–5 years. Religious organisations usually require a minimum contract of 2 years; also, if you wish to be considered for such employment, you not only have to practise your religion but you will be expected to have a degree, professional qualification or practical skills.

Getting a temporary job

You stand a better chance of getting a work permit if you are interested in a **temporary job** or a **working holiday**. In that case, the Embassy concerned will be able to advise you whom you should contact. You can also obtain useful details from publications such as: *Directory of Summer Jobs Abroad* (published by Vacation Work) *Summer Employment Directory of the US* (published by Vacation Work) *Working Holidays* (Central Bureau for Educational Visits and Exchanges.

Voluntary work and exchanges

Then there are voluntary organisations such as TOC H Clayton Volunteers (various programmes in the USA). Also, you might qualify for being considered on an exchange basis for a specified period. Although this type of scheme favours professional people or undergraduates (as part of their educational studies) there is an increasing tendency for other organisations, including youth services and trade unions, to include this experience as part of their training programme.

VOLUNTARY WORK OVERSEAS

If you are unemployed, independent, have some skills and wish to gain experience which should eventually help you get a good job, then you could consider working abroad for a voluntary organisation. Generally you should be over 18 years old (some organisations such as VSO specify age over 20 years) although there are a few programmes which have a minimum age of 17 years.

Although there are more opportunities to work in Third World countries such as Africa, Asia and Latin America, there is a need for volunteers in more developed parts of the world. In such countries invaluable work is done by volunteers representing many well-known national and international voluntary organisations, both religious and non-religious. Some of these are run privately, others partly funded by governments.

Most of these organisations regularly publicise work opportunities in leaflets and notices which give details of the country involved, age range and skills required and minimum duration of contract to be served. As a volunteer you would be regarded as an unpaid worker, entitled to free food and accommodation as well as a regular 'allowance' which, in many instances, would be more than local pay.

Getting more information

If you are interested in doing voluntary work abroad, you can obtain names and addresses of relevant organisations from your Careers Centre, Jobcentre or main library. Rather than write to the organisation concerned, it may be possible to telephone and find out more information from a local representative.

In most areas the Careers Centre regularly produces informative leaflets on voluntary work overseas. These refer to useful publications and give addresses, for example:

* *The International Directory of Voluntary Work* published by Vacation Work.

- *Kibbutz Volunteer* published by Vacation Work.

More importantly, there are details of organisations and specific work areas where volunteers are needed; such as:

- *Missions to Seamen*: St Michael Paternoster Royal, College Hill, London EC4R 2RL. Minimum age 18. Europe, Far East, Australia, Communicant Anglicans, able to swim, with valid driving licence. Minimum six months service.

Having the right attitude

You are likely to be interested in voluntary work overseas if you want to commit yourself for a specified time to helping in a particular programme. The main thing is to ensure you really want to do such work so that, although the money side is insignificant, you will achieve considerable satisfaction from doing a worthwhile job helping others.

WORKING HOLIDAYS ABROAD

As there are currently 30,000 (mainly EU) vacation jobs available, this is an important area for your job search!

Opportunities for students

Nowadays there are many opportunities to earn money by working at the same time as being on holiday abroad. Although most young people who take advantage of this situation are students on higher education courses, these opportunities are open to any unemployed 18–25-year-old. Most probably students on higher education courses are involved because they *know* about such opportunities! Vacation is the only time they can earn money and let's face it, with the decline in the value of grants, most students need to earn extra money to survive. Also, they are encouraged to have a change from the academic life and what better way than to take a working holiday? Reputable leisure organisations go out of their way to encourage applications from such students; consequently there is a mass of information displayed in the college/university library. So, if you fit into this category, as a student/undergraduate on a higher education course, you won't have to search for an address to write to or a form to complete. Just pop into the library!

Finding out information

If, however, you are the average unemployed 18–25-year-old who does not often visit main libraries, it is unlikely that you will see such inviting literature. Of course, you may happen to hear a radio programme about working holidays, in which case you will know how to go about things.

Generally, though, if you *are* interested, you will need to go to a main library to discover in detail what you have to do. You will find there are some good reference books which explain whom to contact. This will involve writing a letter of application, together with your CV and possibly a photograph (some organisations may require this). If your initial approach is satisfactory, you will be asked to complete an application form. In some instances, the application form may consist of several sheets.

What to expect

The type of organisation that offers such holiday employment varies from small firms to large international companies. Some offer first-class training as well as pay, accommodation and food but obviously the 'package' will vary. For example, the pay may be low but the standard of food and accommodation high. Or you may have to accept some discomfort but remember that you are being paid and that, furthermore, you will acquire certain skills and experience which may help you get a permanent job!

CHECKLIST

1. If you intend working in a country which is not in the EU, first contact the Embassy concerned.

2. Make sure you fully understand your employment contract, particularly legal implications and insurance aspects.

3. Find out as much as possible about living conditions – climate, accommodation, *etc*.

4. For further information, see the Further Reading section on page 116.

16
Ethnic Minorities

USING THE SUPPORT AVAILABLE

You should take full advantage of the support facilities available from your particular ethnic group! You may belong to one of the bigger, well-established and more traditional ethnic groups, in which case your life will already be organised in a distinctive way. Or your immediate family may be self-sufficient and run its own business. Either way, you will be able to benefit from the educational and training facilities available to everyone living in Britain.

COMMUNITY GROUPS AND ORGANISATIONS

If necessary, you can widen your contacts through your local **Racial Equality Council**, which represents local ethnic groups as well as a wide range of other organisations – leisure groups, the Red Cross, religious groups, *etc*. Also, you may be lucky enough to be in an area where there are special organisations set up to deal with specific problems such as unemployment. You will be able to get these names and addresses from your local telephone directory. The main thing is for you to find out what facilities are available and how you can benefit from them.

PRESENTING YOURSELF

Without the backing of a community group it will be that much more necessary to follow the advice given in this book. You will notice that one of the main issues concerns presenting yourself in the best possible way. Probably your most effective way to be considered for employment is a 'planned' call at selected business premises. If you take the trouble to plan, as advised in Chapter 10, you will be able to discuss your strengths in relation to the job/work situation and the employer will tend to consider you on your true merits.

It will also be important to remember differences in customs can be misinterpreted. For instance, a modest, downcast look could be thought of as being 'shifty' or evasive. The custom of avoiding eye contact with a stranger may be regarded as indifference. You have only to think of the different forms of greeting all around the world, including kissing on both cheeks and rubbing noses, and you soon realise that there are many ways of getting the message across.

What you have to do is decide beforehand what is likely to be acceptable in your situation. If you are thorough in your approach and think about it carefully, then hopefully, you will be able to present yourself in the best possible way and make the necessary impact to get that job!

GETTING MORE INFORMATION

Visit the library, also your local **Equality Council** and/or **Citizens' Advice Bureau** (see addresses and telephone numbers in the local telephone directory) and find out more about the organisations advertising vacancies which state: 'We welcome applications from Asians, Afro-Caribbean and other black people who are currently under-represented in our work.'

17
Sample Letters

Good letters are perhaps more vital in job-hunting than in any other aspect of daily life. The following pages contain a set of sample letters to cover a range of needs. Try not to follow them slavishly! Develop and refine your own to meet your own specific needs.

- Don't just send off your first draft.
- Read it through and re-draft it if necessary.
- Ask a friend or relative for their comments before you send it off.

When looking at the sample letters shown on the next pages, be **critical**. Get practice in asking yourself these questions, about your own letters:

- Is it addressed to the right person?
- Is it properly laid out (good format) and dated?
- Does it stick to the point?
- Does it sound businesslike and natural?
- Have I made the main points I wanted to?
- Does it sound confident and positive?
- Is the handwriting really clear?
- Is the signature legible, or if not have I printed my name underneath?

And before you rush off to the letterbox with it:

- Have I got someone else to read it through?
- Did I remember all the enclosures?
- Do I need to keep a copy of the letter, and of any enclosures?
- Should I enclose a stamped self-addressed envelope?
- Should it go first class?

Telephone: Bilsden 12045

83 York Road,
Bilsden,
Yorkshire
BY2 9WP

Dear Sir,

20th Mar 9X

I am 16 yrs old and left Bilsden Comprehensive last July. I passed G.C.S.E.s in English, Maths, Woodwork and Technical Drawing which is my best subject.

Next week I complete a training course where I've worked for the Council and gone to the local Tech for Block Release. There is no chance of a job with them so I thought I'd write off to a few employers.

I am good with my hands, don't mind hard work and am quite strong. I help my dad quite a lot at home. My supervisor will give me a good reference about my work and timekeeping.

Will you please consider me for a job. I should be grateful if you could interview me.

Yours truly,

Tim White

Manager,
Tinpot PLC,
Industrial Estate,
Bilsden
Yorkshire BY1 LP2

Fig. 19. Exploratory letter. Comments reflect a good profile with a natural style. However, it is not as informative as it should be concerning the length of the training course, skills acquired and job/work experience details. A typed CV would complement this letter and create the necessary impact.

Tel: Birley 89643

4 Tower Road
Birley
Lancs BL3 9FM

21st April 9X

Dear Mr Lloyd,

As your company usually takes on a few college leavers each year, I thought I would write and enquire whether you are likely to have a suitable vacancy for me.

At present I am on a 2yr Business Studies (BTEC) National Diploma Course which finishes in June this year. If possible, I want to get a job involving computers as I am interested in this field and consider that I can offer some experience.

I attach my C.V. and meanwhile would welcome the opportunity to discuss my career prospects with your organisation.

Yours sincerely
Jane Frodsham

Mr J Lloyd,
Personnel Manager
International Chemicals Ltd,
Birley
BL1 6AR

Fig. 20. Exploratory letter. Has made good use of her knowledge of the company (found out the name of the personnel manager, *etc.*). The letter is also persuasive – it would complement her typed CV and be likely to get the reader to think seriously about seeing her.

REF: JUNIOR ASSISTANT

20 Wogan Road
Mapperly
Nr Dirby
D1J 4TV

Telephone : Dirby 50132

Dear Mr Wood,   5th May 9X

I wish to apply for the above job advertised in today's
Guardian. I left school at Christmas and am
doing a Community Programme which is due to finish
next month. What I am doing is mainly outside
work — gardening and sweeping — but I am used to
answering the phone and would like to do Office work
At present I work for the Council who will give me
good references.
Will you please send me further details and an
application form which I will complete straight away.
Thank you.
Adam Blissett

Mr K. Wood
Manager
Bee Bright Ltd
Main Elm Road
Dirby
D40 AN

Fig. 21. Reply to advert which asked applicants to write for further details
and application form. Prompt reply. Included some useful information about
himself (implied flexibility and direct keenness). Natural 'tone'.

12 Navigation Road
Puddlewich
Nr. Stafford
Staffordshire PQ1 3CS

Ref: Office Junior

Telephone Puddlewich 5812

20th March 199X

Dear Mr. Pears,

I wish to apply for the above-mentioned position.
I am 17 years old, with GCSEs in English Language
(B grade), English Literature (C grade), Maths (C grade),
Commerce (C grade) and French (B grade). At present
I am attending a 1 year Business Studies Course at
the local College of Further Education. This course
finishes in June when I shall be taking BTEC exams
in People & Communication, World of Work, Business
Calculations, Data Processing and RSA Typing Stage II.

Your firm has a good reputation for training young
people and if I am given the opportunity I intend
to work hard and improve my office skills –
particularly typing. The job also appeals to me
because it is in a small, busy office (I think
I would enjoy that !)

I attach my C.V. and hope to hear from you.

Yours sincerely

Margaret Pagdin

Mr. K N Pears
Solicitor
Merrydown Road
Stafford
SL4 1PQ

Fig. 22. Reply to advert. Good immediate impact, although the first paragraph is too lengthy – it seems to be *too* carefully written. The second paragraph is most impressive – reflects her enthusiasm, attitude, aims, *etc*. Should get the writer an interview!

Ref: Vacancy   12 Park Lane,
Trainee VDU Operator   Crispen.
                                                    Nr Alton.
                                                    A21 CY34

                                    Telephone: Alton 70132

Dear Mr Browne,   4th Jun 9X
            I wish to apply for the above post
which was advertised in yesterday's Chronicle.
            I am 18 years old and have GCSEs
in English + Maths as well as 5 others including
Technical Drawing and Geography.
            Since leaving Carlton Comprehensive
I have worked relief at Bungos Warehouse and
done general office work for C.E. Cotes Electrical.
However, I am keen to get a permanent job.
            Your vacancy interests me because I
should get training in something I like dealing
with — computers. Also your company has got a
good reputation and if I am given the opportunity
I shall work hard.
            I am available for interview at any
time. If you phone Mr Elliot at Bungos (Alton 5412)
and Mr Cotes (Alton 9824) they will give me a good
reference.
            Yours sincerely
            Peter Martin

Mr N. Browne
Personnel Manager
A.C.S. Ltd
Alton A34 21N

Fig. 23. Reply to advert. Contents of the letter are informative and well organised, giving a clear profile of Peter. He has written about his strong points in relation to job details (advert also stated preference for GCSE English and Maths); has also given reference phone numbers.

Your ref: NB/AS/Vac

12 Park Lane
Crispen
Nr Alton A21 CY34

Telephone: Alton 70132

8th Jun 9X

Dear Mr Browne,

Thank you for your letter dated 7th Jun inviting me to attend interview on Thursday 11th Jun at 9.30 a.m. for Selection testing.

I understand that it will take all morning and will be pleased to bring my certificates with me when I report to the Training Centre,

Thank you for giving me this opportunity.

Yours sincerely,
Peter Martin

Mr N. Browne
Personnel Manager
A.C.S Ltd
Alton A34 2IN

Fig. 24. Reply to letter requesting interview and certificates. Prompt reply – brief and clear confirmation. Has copied the business format indicated in the company's letter.

Tel: Bestwick 48120

2 Marton Lane
Gawsworth
Nr Bestwick
BK1 30A

19th June 9X

Dear Mrs Brand

Thank you for your letter dated 17th June. I shall be pleased to attend interview on Wednesday 25th June at 10.45 a.m. and will bring my driving licence and copy of my college report. I look forward to seeing you.

Yours sincerely

Allan Stuart

Mrs T. Brand
Staff Manageress
Super-Buy Stores
Bestwick
BK 2PΨ

Fig. 25. Acknowledgement of letter requesting interview. Prompt – brief – clear!

20 Maple Avenue
Bolingbrook
Newton

NB 2 CH

Mr S. Sparkes
Manager
Magnetic Plc.
Barnes Road
Newton N3 4DJ

21st April 9X

Dear Mr Sparkes,

Thank you for your letter dated 16th April. Although disappointed by not being chosen, I was pleased to be short-listed and enjoyed my tour of your factory. I wonder if I can ask you to consider keeping my application on a Waiting List for future employment.

I am not sure if you keep such a list but, if so, I would be most grateful to be considered when you have another vacancy. I really would like to work for your company.

Yours sincerely,

Betty Feather

Fig. 26. Acknowledgement of rejection letter and, at same time, requesting to be put on waiting list. Polite acknowledgement. Request shows keenness to work for company – more important, it can be followed up when there *is* a vacancy.

Mr. D. Wilton,
Manager,
Soft-Toys Ltd.,
39 Parr Road,
Alton A42 1J

12 Park Lane,
Crispen.
Nr Alton.
A21 C734
Telephone: Alton 70132

2nd Jun 9X

Dear Mr Wilton,

Thank you for your letter dated 28th May. I was disappointed at not being accepted for the job - however, I am pleased that you have written about putting me on your Waiting List.

I would still like to work for your company and hope to get the chance to do so I will be very pleased if you put my name on your Waiting List and understand that this is without commitment on either part.

Thank you for seeing me last week.

Yours sincerely,
Peter Martin

P.S. I have showed my parents your letter and they are pleased too!

Fig. 27. Reply to letter asking if you want to be put on waiting list, without commitment on either part (yours or employer's). Prompt reply – natural tone (disappointed at not getting the job for which he was interviewed but still keen to work there).

30 Elm Road
Sipley
Derbyshire
SD2 0LL

Mr B Blunt
Manager
Y.S. Poat Ltd
Sipley
S 20 4JK

4th April 9X

Dear Mr Blunt,

Thank you for your letter dated 3rd April together with contract of employment.

I am pleased to accept your offer and have signed the copy of the Employment Contract which I enclose with this letter.

I will be pleased to report to the Personnel Department at 9 a.m. on Monday 14th April 9X.

Yours sincerely,
Alice Browne

Fig. 28. Handwritten letter of acceptance of job – to be sent with signed copy of contract of employment. Prompt – brief – clear – polite! Although it is not necessary to send this type of letter, it gives a good impression.

Useful Addresses

Association of British Correspondence Colleges, 6 Francis Grove, London SW19 4DT.

BBC Education Department, BBC TV Centre, Centre House, 56 Wood Lane, London W12 7SB.

Career Analysts, Career House, 90 Gloucester Place, London W1H 4BL.

Careers & Occupational Information Centre, Moorfoot, Sheffield S1 4PQ.

Careers & Occupational Information Centre, 5 Kirkloan, Corstorphine, Edinburgh EH12 7HD.

Careers Research & Advisory Centre (CRAC), Sheraton House, Castle Park, Cambridge CB3 0AX.

Central Bureau for Educational Visits & Exchanges (CBEVE), 10 Spring Gardens, London SW1A 2BN.

Central Council for Education & Training in Social Work, Derbyshire House, St Chad's Street, London WC1H 8AD; South Gate House, Wood Street, Cardiff, CF1 1ES; 70/80 George Street, Edinburgh EH2 3BU; 6 Malone Road, Belfast BT9 5BN.

Central Office of Information, Hercules Road, London SE1 7DU.

Concordia (Youth Service Volunteers), 8 Brunswick Place, Hove, East Sussex BN3 1ET.

Engineering Council, 10 Maltravers Street, London WC2R 3ER.

Hotel Careers Centre, 43 Norwich Avenue West, Bournemouth BH2 6AJ.

Hotel & Catering Training Company, International House, High Street, London W5 5DB.

Independent Schools Careers Organisation, 12a/18a Princess Way, Camberley, Surrey GU15 3SP.

International Christian Youth Exchange, c/o Church of England Youth Services, Church House, Great Smith Street, London SW1P 3NZ.

Kibbutz Representatives, 1a Accommodation Road, London NW11 8ED.

Mission to Seamen, St Michael's Paternoster Royal, College Hill, London EC4R 2RL.

Outward Bound Trust, Watermillock, Nr Penrith, Cumbria CA11 0JL.

Overseas Placing Unit, Employment Service, Rockingham House, 123 West Street, Sheffield S1 4ER.

Passport Office, Clive House, 70–78 Petty France, London SW1H 9HD. (Application forms from main post offices, travel agents, Lloyds Bank.)

Prince's Trust, The, 18 Park Square East, London NW1 4LH.

Race Relations/Racial Equality: consult your local ethnic group.

Royal College of Nursing, 20 Cavendish Square, London W1M 0AB.

Sports Council, 16 Upper Woburn Place, London WC1H 0QP.

Vacation Work, 9 Park End Street, Oxford OX1 1JH.

Voluntary Service Overseas, 317 Putney Bridge Road, London SW15 2PN.

Youth Exchange Council, The British Council, 10 Spring Gardens, London SW1A 2BN.

See your local telephone directory for:

Citizens' Advice Bureaux
Leisure centres
Libraries
Sports centres.

Glossary

Action Line programmes: radio or TV programmes which involve 'live' participants – people who take part without any rehearsal, speaking about some (usually controversial) major topic of the moment.

Apprenticeship: the time of training for a trade or craft, *eg* engineering, bricklaying, formally agreed between employer and employee. (See also **Modern Apprenticeships**.)

Aptitude test: exercises you complete within a fixed time to discover what kind of work you are likely to do well at.

Benefits: money you can claim (*eg* Jobseeker's Allowance) whilst seeking work.

Citizens' Advice Bureaux (CABx): a national organisation with local branches, staffed by trained volunteers who give advice and help to people with problems.

Correspondence course: studying by postal communication rather than face-to-face teaching.

Counselling: service given by someone trained to advise on various matters, *eg* careers.

CV (curriculum vitae): means 'course of life' – used when applying for jobs, giving brief personal details: name, address, telephone number, age, education, qualifications, work experience, interests/hobbies.

Employment Training Adviser: based in Jobcentre; helps you look for work and advises on the type of training programme and the benefits you can claim whilst looking for a job.

Health and Safety Regulations: legal requirements for health and safety of employees at work, as defined by the government.

Jobclub: government-funded, set up in areas of high unemployment to assist groups of long-term unemployed in concentrated job search.

Job market: existing job vacancies.

Jobseeker's Agreement: agreement signed jointly by you and your Employment Service Adviser when you claim Jobseeker's Allowance.

Jobseeker's Allowance: benefit you receive when you sign a Jobseeker's Agreement.

Job specification: a brief description of job responsibilities and tasks involved.

Modern Apprenticeships: training schemes lasting 3–5 years leading to high levels of skills and qualifications (NVQs) working within sectors such as information technology and retail as well as traditional industries.

NVQs (National Vocational Qualifications): practically based qualifications designed to meet national standards required by industry. They are awarded at 5 different levels, each one indicating a particular level of competence, with the top level (5) involving substantial personal accountability such as management of other managers.

Open Learning: flexible learning with programme tailored to suit individual needs. You can learn at your own pace at a time and place to suit you (home, work, Open College's access centres).

Personal details: (in relation to employment) basic facts about you – full name, address, telephone number, age, education, qualifications, work experience.

Personal profile: brief information about yourself.

Referee: someone who provides a personal recommendation to support your application for a job.

Role play: taking part in an imagined situation, *eg* employment interview.

Self-employment: work for yourself – be your own boss.

Self-assessment: judging your own abilities – strong points and areas to be improved upon.

Service company: organisation which sells a service rather than manufacturing goods, *eg* insurance, banks.

Skillcentre: training workshop where you are given intensive instruction in a particular skill.

Take-home pay: net pay – the actual amount of money you take home after all deductions, *eg* Income Tax, National Insurance contributions.

TAPS (Training Access Points): helps you identify training opportunities which best meet your needs. Provides quick access to education and training information through computer-backed TAPS located in Jobcentres, public libraries and Careers Centres.

TECs (Training and Enterprise Councils): operate on a regional basis with direct accountability to the Department of Education and Employment. They work closely with all Careers Centres and

Jobcentrès as well as employers and training providers to guide the development of careers education and help co-ordinate quality training related to job opportunities within the locality.

Vocational guidance: advice about work appropriate to your personal qualities and abilities.

VSO (Voluntary Service Overseas): an international organisation which employs volunteers who have suitable skills to work overseas, mostly in under-developed countries.

Youth training: formal government training for young people.

Further Reading

USEFUL BOOKS

Career choices
Decisions at 15/16+.
GNVQ – Is It For You?
Both published by CRAC (Careers Research and Advisory Centre).

Careers Series. Published by Kogan Page. Books on individual careers
 – Art & Design, Secretarial and Office Work, and others.

Finding a Job in Computers, Stephen Harding.
Getting into Films and Television, Robert Angell.
How to Become an Au Pair, Mark Hempshell.
How to Get into Radio, Bernie Simmons.
How to Work in an Office, Sheila Payne.
How to Work in Retail, Sylvia Lichfield and Christine Hall.
How to Work with Dogs, Pauline Appleby.
Working as a Holiday Rep, Steve Marks.
Working in Hotels and Catering, Mark Hempshell.
Working in Photography, Henry Lewes.
Working in Travel and Tourism, Mark Hempshell.
Working on Cruise Ships, Steve Marks.
Working with Horses, Jenny Morgan.
 All published by How To Books.

Vacation work
Summer Jobs in Britain.
Summer Jobs Abroad.
Summer Employment Directory of the US.
 All published by Vacation Work, 9 Park End Street, Oxford OX1
1JH.

Working abroad

Doing Voluntary Work Abroad, Mark Hempshell.
How to Find Temporary Work Abroad, Nick Vandome.
How to Get a Job Abroad Roger Jones.
How to Get a Job in Europe, Mark Hempshell.
How to Get a Job in France, Mark Hempshell.
How to Get a Job in Germany, Christine Hall.
How to Live and Work in Germany, Christine Hall.
Living and Working in the Netherlands, Pat Rush.
How to Spend a Year Abroad, Nick Vandome.
This is a selection of How To Books on Living and Working Abroad. For a complete list, send for a copy of the latest catalogue (see back cover for details).

Directory of Jobs and Careers Abroad.
Kibbutz Volunteer.
International Directory of Voluntary Work.
Directory of Work and Study in Developing Countries.
All published by Vacation Work, 9 Park End Street, Oxford OX1 1JH.

Other useful books

Go for It – The Essential Guide to Opportunities for Young People, Martyn Lewis (Lennard Publishing).
The Gap Year Guidebook, Rosamund McDougall (Peridot Press).

USEFUL INFORMATION

Make full use of the local services which affect your job search plan – you need to be aware of the job market!

Leaflets

These often become out of date and are replaced. Get into the habit of regularly looking at leaflets in Careers Centres, Jobcentres, libraries, leisure clubs and post offices. The following are all extremely useful:

Just The Job.
Jobseeker's Allowance – Helping You Back to Work.
Back to Work Benefits.
Young People's Guide to Social Security.
Available from Jobcentres, Benefits Offices, post offices.

Working in Another Country of the European Union. Published by the European Commission. Available in the Business Section of main public libraries or from your local MEP – see telephone directory).

Notices
Noticeboards in schools, colleges, Careers Centres, Jobcentres and libraries are often *full* and it is easy to overlook important information which affects your job search. Don't rely on the 'eye-catching' notices – you might miss something like:

Camp America – enrolment meeting – 400 vacancies

Local newspapers – including free ones!
As well as the **vacancies** pages, try to 'spot' items that might interest you, such as an **article** about a new company moving into your area or **news** that the local council is extending a work experience scheme for 15–16-year-olds, involving an advertising campaign, seeking sponsorship from local companies, using office equipment, *etc.* – for those who want to succeed despite leaving school without qualifications (what about that!)

Advertisements
Try to 'spot' adverts that could affect your job search plan, such as an Open Day for a local college, or a Work Fair organised by the TEC and local Chamber of Commerce, where many companies will be represented.

Index

LEARNING NEW JOB SKILLS
How and where to obtain the right training to help you get on at work

Laurel Alexander

Did you know there is a skills shortage out in the workplace? There are literally hundreds of well-paid vacancies waiting for the right person who is properly trained. This book presents a positive approach to education and training and will enable you to make considered and informed choices about improving your job prospects. Taking a training course will improve your confidence, prepare you for a job with a future, potentially increase your earnings and bring fresh challenge back into your life. Discover how to train for the service industry and fulfil the skills shortage. There is information on how to get into university without any prior qualifications, the benefits of learning at home and how to make use of the NVQ system. There are guidelines on how to get funding for training courses, getting vocational training if you are unemployed and returning to study as a mature student. Learning is for everyone – and this is the book to give you the confidence to go for it. Laurel Alexander is a specialist trainer and writer in career development and has helped hundreds of adults improve their working lives.

128pp illus. 1 85703 375 2.

HOW TO WORK FROM HOME
A practical handbook for the independent professional

Ian Phillipson

Here is a complete step-by-step guide to successful planning and organisation of what is fast becoming the preferred option for millions of individuals in the new work environment of the 1990s. 'A wonderful book written by a man with a splendid sense of humour and a good practical approach. It concentrates on the key techniques that will make you really efficient yet comfortable when working from home, and able to compete on equal terms with even the most efficient firms and organisations.' *Home Run Magazine.*

176pp illus. 1 85703 158 X. 2nd edition.

WRITING A CV THAT WORKS
Developing and using your key marketing tool

Paul McGee

What makes a CV stand out from the crowd? How can you present yourself in the most successful way? This practical book shows you how to develop different versions of your CV for every situation. Reveal your hidden skills, identify your achievements and learn how to communicate these successfully. Different styles and uses for a CV are examined, as you discover the true importance of your most powerful marketing tool. Paul McGee is a freelance Trainer and Consultant for one of Britain's largest out-placement organisations. He conducts Marketing Workshops for people from all walks of life.

128pp illus. 1 85703 365 5. 2nd edition.

PASSING THAT INTERVIEW
Your step-by-step guide to achieving success

Judith Johnstone

Everyone knows how to shine at interview – or do they? When every candidate becomes the perfect clone of the one before, you have to have that extra 'something' to raise your chances above the rest. Using a systematic and practical approach, this **How To** book takes you step-by-step through the essential pre-interview ground-work, the interview encounter itself, and what you can learn from the experience afterwards. The book contains sample pre- and post-interview correspondence, and is complete with a guide to further reading, glossary of terms, and index. 'This is from the first class How To Books stable.' *Escape Committee Newsletter.* 'Offers a fresh approach to a well documented subject.' *Newscheck/Careers Service Bulletin.* 'A complete step-by-step guide.' *The Association of Business Executives.* Judith Johnstone is a Graduate of the Institute of Personnel & Development; she has been an instructor in Business Studies and adult literacy tutor, and has long experience of helping people at work.

144 pp illus. 1 85703 360 4. 4th edition.

CAREER NETWORKING
How to develop the right contacts to help you throughout your working life

Laurel Alexander

Unemployed? Redundant? Wanting promotion? – then career networking is for you. By systematically networking with other people, you can build bridges which could bring in offers of work. This book helps you take control of your working life through setting goals, assessing your networking needs and cultivating a supportive network. By working step-by-step through each practical chapter, you will understand how you can develop and plan your career through other people. Discover how you can be seen as a specialist selling something everyone wants using effective communication skills, assertive behaviour and being seen as a positive person. Learn how to network a room, how to gather information anywhere, from anyone. Do you know how to network using E-mail, the Internet and other technology? This book tells you how. There is further information on starting your own network, getting on other people's networks and extending your network. Laurel Alexander is a freelance trainer and consultant in career development and has helped many individuals improve their working life.

136pp illus. 1 85703 350 7.

HOW TO MARKET YOURSELF
A practical guide to winning at work

Ian Phillipson

In today's intensely competitive workplace it has become ever more vital to market yourself effectively, whether as a first-time job hunter, existing employee, or mature returner. This hard-hitting new manual provides a really positive step-by-step guide to assessing yourself, choosing the right personal image, identifying and presenting the right skills, building confidence, marketing yourself in person and on paper, organising your self-marketing campaign, using mentors at work, selling yourself to colleagues, clients and customers, and marketing yourself for a fast-changing future. The book is complete with assignments and case studies.

160pp illus. 1 85703 160 1.

HOW TO WORK IN AN OFFICE
Getting off to a successful start

Sheila Payne

Thousands of school/college leavers – and mature returners – go to work in offices every year. But what exactly is an office? What functions does it perform? What tasks need to be done? With its clearly written text, examples and short case studies, this helpful book will provide an excellent preparation for everyone entering the world of office work for the first time. 'Continues the excellent standard of previous How To Books . . . an essential addition to any public or school library.' *Careers Guidance Today*. Sheila Payne is an office skills trainer; she holds teacher's diplomas in typewriting and word-processing, and the City & Guilds Youth Trainers Award/Vocational Assessors Award.

160pp illus 1 85703 094 X.

CAREER PLANNING FOR WOMEN
How to make a positive impact on your working life

Laurel Alexander

More women are entering the workplace than ever before. Whether it is on the corporate ladder or self employed, women are establishing a much stronger place for themselves within the world of commerce and industry. As global and national markets shift and business ethos develops, the specific qualities of women play a vital part alongside those of men. Business has been influenced primarily by male thought and action. Now there is the opportunity for women to make a substantial contribution with new ideas and approaches. The book is not about women taking men's jobs or about women being better or worse than men. It is intended to help women understand their unique and emerging role in business, change their perception of themselves and take much more responsibility for their responses and actions within the work-place. Laurel Alexander is a manager/trainer in career development who has helped many individuals succeed in changing their work direction.

160pp illus. 1 85703 417 1.

HOW TO RETURN TO WORK
Building new skills, new confidence and a new career

Ann Dobson

Are you thinking of returning to work after time away? If so, this is the book for you. In clear steps, it advises you how to enter today's market, how to review and update your skills, and how to succeed in job applications and interviews. Use it to discover new self-confidence, learn how to deal effectively with a new boss, new colleagues and a new work environment. With its helpful checklists, self-assessment material and revealing case studies, this positive book shows you how you can really develop your potential and build a whole new future for yourself. Ann Dobson is Principal of a Secretarial Training School with long experience of helping people prepare themselves for work. She is also author of *How to Communicate at Work* and *Writing Business Letters* in this series.

128pp illus. 1 85703 144 X.

GETTING YOUR FIRST JOB
How to win the offer of good prospects and a regular pay packet

Penny Hitchin

It's a tough world for jobhunters – especially for those with no track record. The days when newcomers to the job market could walk into 'A job for life' have gone. Jobseekers today must impress a potential employer with their personal qualities and attitudes as well as their paper qualifications. Once in work, they must show themselves to be willing, adaptable and flexible – able to learn new skills quickly and cope with constant change. This readable handbook offers young people a real insight into what employers are looking for, encouraging the reader to take a constructive and positive approach to finding their first job. The book includes lots of practical examples, self-assessment material and typical case studies. Penny Hitchin has run Jobfinder programmes and written careers books and materials for TV and radio campaigns on training and employment.

160pp illus. 1 85703 300 0.

HOW TO START A NEW CAREER
Managing a better future for yourself

Judith Johnstone

More people than ever before are faced with big career changes today. Few if any jobs are 'for life'. Now in its second edition, this How To book helps you manage your entry into a new career effectively. It is aimed at anyone making a new start, whatever his or her age or background. It looks at who you are and what you are. It helps you evaluate your life skills, to recognise which careers you should concentrate on, and how to make a realistic plan for a happy and productive future. 'Written very much in the style of a work book, with practical exercises and pro formas for the student to complete ... Well written – would be a useful addition to the library of any guidance practitioner working with adults.' *Newscheck/Careers Service Bulletin.*

140pp illus 1 85703 139 3. 2nd edition.

FINDING A JOB WITH A FUTURE
How to identify and work in growth industries and services

Laurel Alexander

Are you seeking to change your career? Have you been made redundant? Are you returning to work? If you want to ensure a long lasting career move in the right direction, you need to read this book which sets out in a practical way, growth areas of industry and commerce. Discover the work cycle of the future based on job specific skills, abstract skills, continuous learning and life-time career planning. Learn about flexible ways of working. There is occupational information on IT, training and education, business services, leisure, the entertainment industry, social and cultural fields, security and protective services, science and working for the environment. There are job and personal self assessments for each section, plus where to go for training and how to find the jobs. Laurel Alexander is a manager/trainer in career development who has helped many individuals succeed in changing their work direction.

144pp illus. 1 85703 310 8.

How To Books

How To Books provide practical help on a large range of topics. They are available through all good bookshops or can be ordered direct from the distributors. Just tick the titles you want and complete the form on the following page.

___ Apply to an Industrial Tribunal (£7.99)
___ Applying for a Job (£8.99)
___ Applying for a United States Visa (£15.99)
___ Backpacking Round Europe (£8.99)
___ Be a Freelance Journalist (£8.99)
___ Be a Freelance Secretary (£8.99)
___ Become a Freelance Sales Agent (£9.99)
___ Become an Au Pair (£8.99)
___ Becoming a Father (£8.99)
___ Buy & Run a Shop (£8.99)
___ Buy & Run a Small Hotel (£8.99)
___ Buying a Personal Computer (£9.99)
___ Career Networking (£8.99)
___ Career Planning for Women (£8.99)
___ Cash from your Computer (£9.99)
___ Choosing a Nursing Home (£9.99)
___ Choosing a Package Holiday (£8.99)
___ Claim State Benefits (£9.99)
___ Collecting a Debt (£9.99)
___ Communicate at Work (£7.99)
___ Conduct Staff Appraisals (£7.99)
___ Conducting Effective Interviews (£8.99)
___ Coping with Self Assessment (£9.99)
___ Copyright & Law for Writers (£8.99)
___ Counsel People at Work (£7.99)
___ Creating a Twist in the Tale (£8.99)
___ Creative Writing (£9.99)
___ Critical Thinking for Students (£8.99)
___ Dealing with a Death in the Family (£9.99)
___ Do Voluntary Work Abroad (£8.99)
___ Do Your Own Advertising (£8.99)
___ Do Your Own PR (£8.99)
___ Doing Business Abroad (£10.99)
___ Doing Business on the Internet (£12.99)
___ Emigrate (£9.99)
___ Employ & Manage Staff (£8.99)
___ Find Temporary Work Abroad (£8.99)
___ Finding a Job in Canada (£9.99)
___ Finding a Job in Computers (£8.99)
___ Finding a Job in New Zealand (£9.99)
___ Finding a Job with a Future (£8.99)
___ Finding Work Overseas (£9.99)
___ Freelance DJ-ing (£8.99)
___ Freelance Teaching & Tutoring (£9.99)
___ Get a Job Abroad (£10.99)
___ Get a Job in America (£9.99)
___ Get a Job in Australia (£9.99)
___ Get a Job in Europe (£9.99)
___ Get a Job in France (£9.99)
___ Get a Job in Travel & Tourism (£8.99)
___ Get into Radio (£8.99)
___ Getting into Films & Television (£10.99)

___ Getting That Job (£8.99)
___ Getting your First Job (£8.99)
___ Going to University (£8.99)
___ Helping your Child to Read (£8.99)
___ How to Study & Learn (£8.99)
___ Investing in People (£9.99)
___ Investing in Stocks & Shares (£9.99)
___ Keep Business Accounts (£7.99)
___ Know Your Rights at Work (£8.99)
___ Live & Work in America (£9.99)
___ Live & Work in Australia (£12.99)
___ Live & Work in Germany (£9.99)
___ Live & Work in Greece (£9.99)
___ Live & Work in Italy (£8.99)
___ Live & Work in New Zealand (£9.99)
___ Live & Work in Portugal (£9.99)
___ Live & Work in the Gulf (£9.99)
___ Living & Working in Britain (£8.99)
___ Living & Working in China (£9.99)
___ Living & Working in Hong Kong (£10.99)
___ Living & Working in Israel (£10.99)
___ Living & Working in Saudi Arabia (£12.99)
___ Living & Working in the Netherlands (£9.99)
___ Making a Complaint (£8.99)
___ Making a Wedding Speech (£8.99)
___ Manage a Sales Team (£8.99)
___ Manage an Office (£8.99)
___ Manage Computers at Work (£8.99)
___ Manage People at Work (£8.99)
___ Manage Your Career (£8.99)
___ Managing Budgets & Cash Flows (£9.99)
___ Managing Meetings (£8.99)
___ Managing Your Personal Finances (£8.99)
___ Managing Yourself (£8.99)
___ Market Yourself (£8.99)
___ Master Book-Keeping (£8.99)
___ Mastering Business English (£8.99)
___ Master GCSE Accounts (£8.99)
___ Master Public Speaking (£8.99)
___ Migrating to Canada (£12.99)
___ Obtaining Visas & Work Permits (£9.99)
___ Organising Effective Training (£9.99)
___ Pass Exams Without Anxiety (£7.99)
___ Passing That Interview (£8.99)
___ Plan a Wedding (£7.99)
___ Planning Your Gap Year (£8.99)
___ Prepare a Business Plan (£8.99)
___ Publish a Book (£9.99)
___ Publish a Newsletter (£9.99)
___ Raise Funds & Sponsorship (£7.99)
___ Rent & Buy Property in France (£9.99)
___ Rent & Buy Property in Italy (£9.99)

How To Books

___ Research Methods (£8.99)
___ Retire Abroad (£8.99)
___ Return to Work (£7.99)
___ Run a Voluntary Group (£8.99)
___ Setting up Home in Florida (£9.99)
___ Spending a Year Abroad (£8.99)
___ Start a Business from Home (£7.99)
___ Start a New Career (£6.99)
___ Starting to Manage (£8.99)
___ Starting to Write (£8.99)
___ Start Word Processing (£8.99)
___ Start Your Own Business (£8.99)
___ Study Abroad (£8.99)
___ Study & Live in Britain (£7.99)
___ Studying at University (£8.99)
___ Studying for a Degree (£8.99)
___ Successful Grandparenting (£8.99)
___ Successful Mail Order Marketing (£9.99)
___ Successful Single Parenting (£8.99)
___ Survive Divorce (£8.99)
___ Surviving Redundancy (£8.99)
___ Taking in Students (£8.99)
___ Taking on Staff (£8.99)
___ Taking Your A-Levels (£8.99)
___ Teach Abroad (£8.99)
___ Teach Adults (£8.99)
___ Teaching Someone to Drive (£8.99)
___ Travel Round the World (£8.99)
___ Understand Finance at Work (£8.99)
___ Use a Library (£7.99)

___ Use the Internet (£9.99)
___ Winning Consumer Competitions (£8.99)
___ Winning Presentations (£8.99)
___ Work from Home (£8.99)
___ Work in an Office (£7.99)
___ Work in Retail (£8.99)
___ Work with Dogs (£8.99)
___ Working Abroad (£14.99)
___ Working as a Holiday Rep (£9.99)
___ Working in Japan (£10.99)
___ Working in Photography (£8.99)
___ Working in the Gulf (£10.99)
___ Working in Hotels & Catering (£9.99)
___ Working on Contract Worldwide (£9.99)
___ Working on Cruise Ships (£9.99)
___ Write a Press Release (£9.99)
___ Write a Report (£8.99)
___ Write an Assignment (£8.99)
___ Write & Sell Computer Software (£9.99)
___ Write for Publication (£8.99)
___ Write for Television (£8.99)
___ Writing a CV that Works (£8.99)
___ Writing a Non Fiction Book (£9.99)
___ Writing an Essay (£8.99)
___ Writing & Publishing Poetry (£9.99)
___ Writing & Selling a Novel (£8.99)
___ Writing Business Letters (£8.99)
___ Writing Reviews (£9.99)
___ Writing Your Dissertation (£8.99)

To: Plymbridge Distributors Ltd, Plymbridge House, Estover Road, Plymouth PL6 7PZ.
Customer Services Tel: (01752) 202301. Fax: (01752) 202331.

Please send me copies of the titles I have indicated. Please add postage & packing
(UK £1, Europe including Eire, £2, World £3 airmail).

☐ I enclose cheque/PO payable to Plymbridge Distributors Ltd for £ [   ]

☐ Please charge to my ☐ MasterCard, ☐ Visa, ☐ AMEX card.

Account No. [   ]

Card Expiry Date [   ] 19   ☎ Credit Card orders may be faxed or phoned.

Customer Name (CAPITALS) ....

Address ....

.... Postcode ....

Telephone .... Signature ....

Every effort will be made to despatch your copy as soon as possible but to avoid possible
disappointment please allow up to 21 days for despatch time (42 days if overseas). Prices
and availability are subject to change without notice. [Code BPA]